AFTER THE BLAST

AN AUSTRALIAN OFFICER IN IRAQ AND AFGHANISTAN

GARTH CALLENDER

Black Inc.

Published by Black Inc.,
an imprint of Schwartz Publishing Pty Ltd
37–39 Langridge Street
Collingwood VIC 3066 Australia
enquiries@blackincbooks.com
www.blackincbooks.com

National Library of Australia Cataloguing-in-Publication entry:
Callender, Garth, author.
After the blast : An Australian officer in Iraq and Afghanistan / Garth Callender.
9781863957380 (paperback)
9781925203301 (ebook)
Callender, Garth.
Soldiers – Australia – Biography.
Iraq War, 2003–2011 – Personal narratives, Australian.
Iraq War, 2003–2011 – Participation, Australian.
Afghan War, 2001 – Personal narratives, Australian.
Afghan War, 2001 – Participation, Australian.
355.0092

Cover and text design by Peter Long
Cover image: Garth Callender

FSC
www.fsc.org
MIX
Paper from responsible sources
FSC® C009448

Printed in Australia by Griffin Press. The paper this book is printed on is certified against the Forest Stewardship Council® Standards. Griffin Press holds FSC chain of custody certification SGS-COC-005088. FSC promotes environmentally responsible, socially beneficial and economically viable management of the world's forests.

CONTENTS

TURKEY
SYRIA
IRAN
IRAQ
JORDAN
SAUDI
ARABIA
KUWAIT
Al Kasik
Tal Afar
Mosul
Highway 1
Tigris River
Tikrit
Samara
Balad
Baqubah
Kirkush
Falluja
Euphrates River
Baghdad
Ali al Salem Air base
Kuwait
N

Map A: Iraq

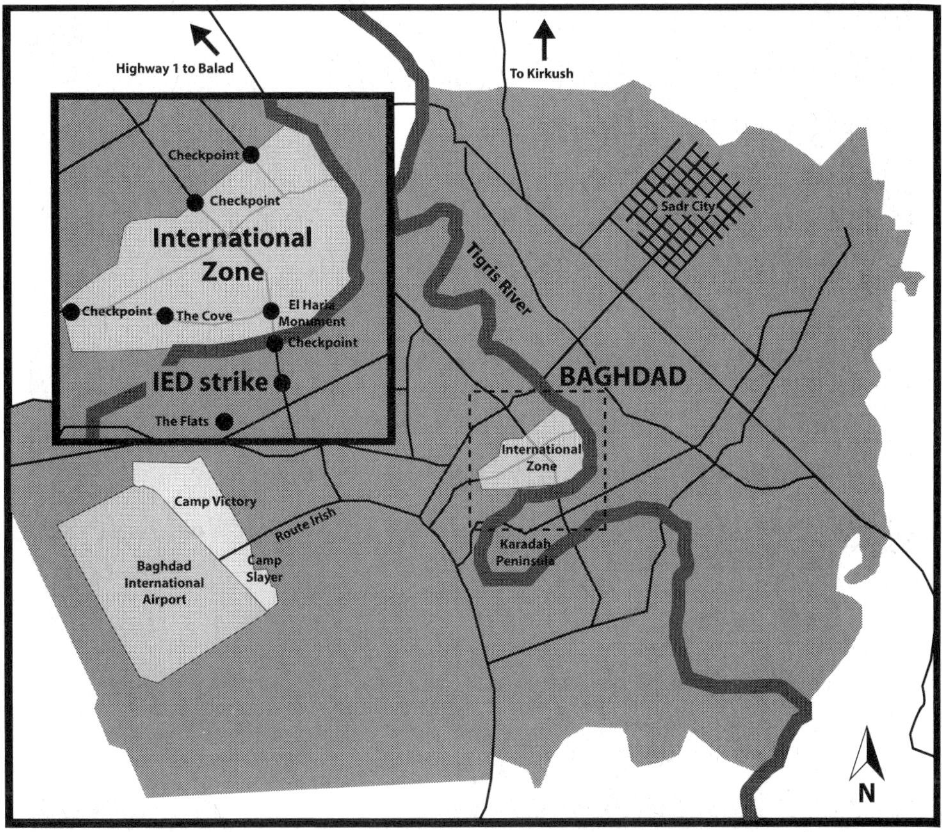

Map B: Baghdad, 2004

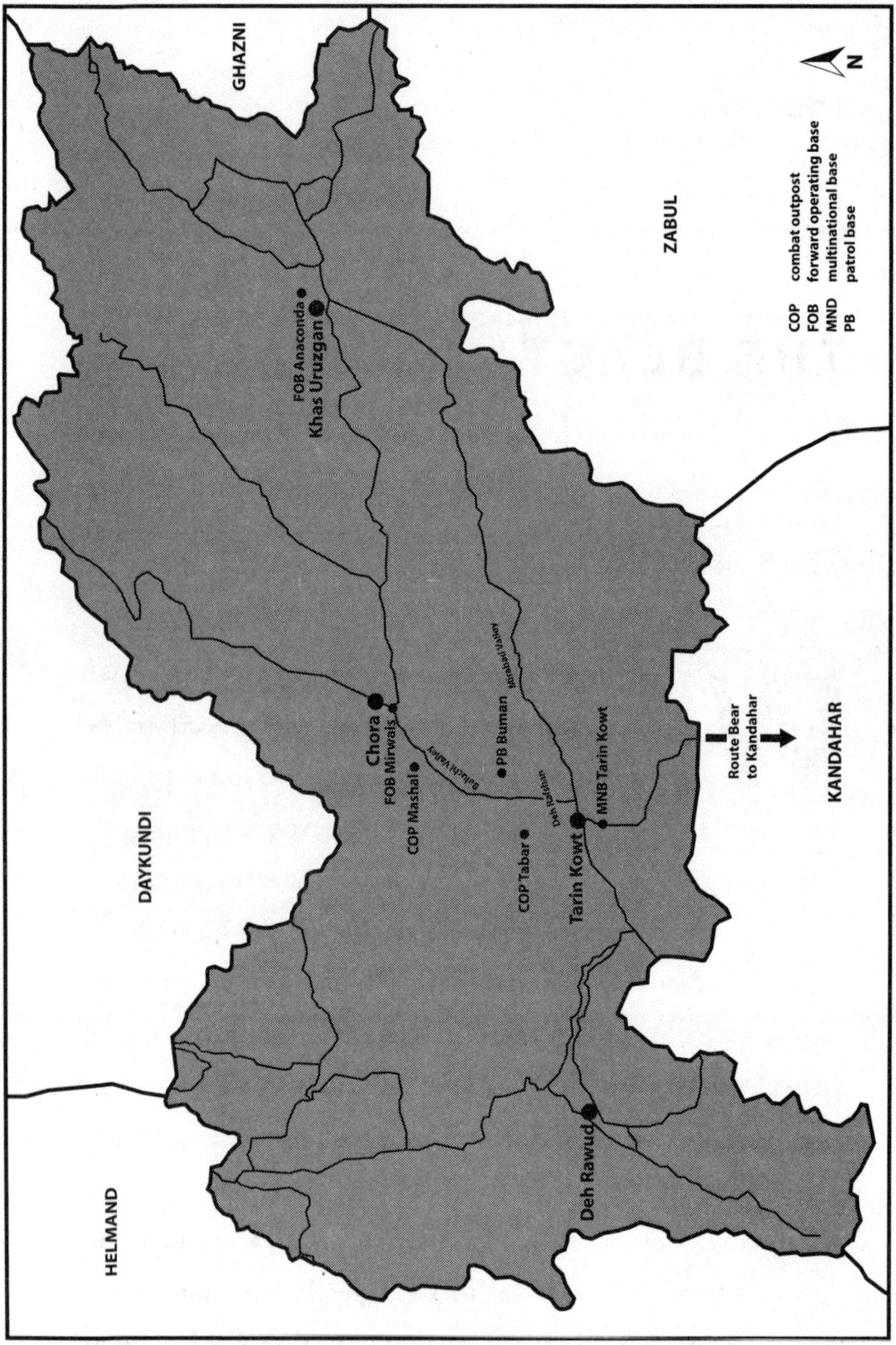

Map C: Uruzgan province, Afghanistan

PROLOGUE

THE BLAST

25 OCTOBER 2004

WE CAME OUT OF THE ROUNDABOUT AND accelerated hard on the road leading north to the checkpoint into the International Zone. I was in the second of two armoured vehicles in convoy, standing up in the turret. The buildings to our right had been noted several times by our intelligence guys as a trouble spot. This morning nothing seemed out of the ordinary. We had no indication that some time earlier an insurgent had parked a car with a cargo of artillery rounds wired to a remote control. There was no sign that, as my vehicle passed it, the device would be triggered by someone overlooking the road.

Of the explosion I remember nothing. I have no recollection of the blast that tore off my helmet and goggles – nothing of how my vehicle lost control and careered into, and uprooted, a tree in the median strip.

I must have been unconscious for only a few seconds. I came to with the thought that I had been shot in the head . . . I was confused, and pissed off, and everything hurt.

I instinctively reached for my head. Although alarmed to find no helmet, I was a little comforted by the fact that I didn't find the gaping hole I'd expected. But I knew I was in trouble, as I couldn't breathe or see and had a terrible pain in my legs. I couldn't get any air into my lungs, and I tried to yell. Nothing came out.

On the second attempt, I managed to let out a whimper, and, though very winded, managed to keep drawing painful breaths after that. I fumbled through the blood and damaged flesh that constituted my eyebrows and the bridge of my nose, and for a second managed to prise open my eyes and look down at the dusty floor of the turret . . .

PART I:
IRAQ
2004

1

WAITING TO DEPLOY

IN MY LAST SIX MONTHS AT MILITARY COLLEGE, planes hit the World Trade Center towers.

A year and a half later, with the fall of Saddam Hussein's regime in April 2003, the job of protecting the Australian embassy in Iraq fell to the Australian army. As a new troop leader in the 2nd Cavalry Regiment based in Darwin, I looked on with envy as the first troop to deploy packed and left in a flurry of activity and repressed excitement. While most of us knew what was going on, there was a security requirement to keep our mouths shut, so the troop left under a cover of quasi-secrecy.

Seventeen months later I would get my chance to deploy.

*

Even though I had served for almost eight years, my military career up until deployment had been unexceptional. I had joined as a directionless nineteen-year-old looking for adventure. The boy who joined in 1996 as an infantry rifleman never expected to end up in Iraq or Afghanistan as an officer.

I joined a peacetime army where the opportunities for real operational experience were extremely rare. A few years after joining, I somehow impressed my commanding officer during a field training exercise and was recommended for officer training at the Royal Military College, Duntroon.

I started at Duntroon with the naive belief that I could live the same lifestyle I had as a soldier and somehow coast through the eighteen-month course. So the only really exceptional thing about my early career was the extensive conduct record I accumulated during officer training. Drinking when on the dry, sleeping through parade, turning in work that wasn't my own – ten charges in total. These charges saw me spend far too much of my time marching around the parade ground on misty mornings and bitter, cold Canberra evenings. With the later offences, the prosecutor would make a point of dropping my conduct record on the desk of the officer hearing the charge so that the house-brick thick document would make a dramatic thud as it landed.

Luckily, I got serious about my career about the same time the world got serious for my generation. It wasn't just 9/11; a lot of things focused and shaped my new attitude. I applied to be allocated to armoured corps, specifically cavalry, as I had a gut feeling I could achieve the most commanding a troop of vehicles and soldiers. Such teams had, by that time, already done well in East Timor, and had a proud history, from the Boer War through to Vietnam. So, with new-found drive and motivation, I focused on military studies at the college and ended up graduating in the top 15 per cent of the class, and was given my preference of corps and posting.

After graduating from Duntroon as a young lieutenant, I was posted to the 2nd Cavalry Regiment, then the only unit that had ASLAVs (Australian Light Armoured Vehicles). I spent my first year bouncing around the country completing courses so I could do my job commanding thirty soldiers and six vehicles: six months vehicle training in Puckapunyal, Victoria, and range qualifications in Singleton, New South Wales. This was followed by numerous field-training exercises throughout the Northern Territory and Queensland to further learn all I could about the very technically and tactically challenging job of being a cavalry troop leader.

In the middle of it all I almost got sent to sea for four months to help the navy with illegal immigrant ships – luckily I was saved at the last minute by my commanding officer, who thought I could be better employed.

*

My first deployment to Baghdad was with the fifth rotation of the Australian Security Detachment to Iraq. Colloquially known as SECDET V, it was a group of about 110 soldiers commanded by an infantry major. We would leave Australia in early September 2004 for a four-month rotation. In the first two months we would protect the embassy, so that the staff there could carry out their diplomatic work as safely as possible. We would spend the second two months in northern Iraq, providing protection to Australians who were helping train an Iraqi army brigade.

We trained specifically for Iraq for four months, all through the Darwin wet season. Four months training for a four-month deployment – there was something a little 'over-cooked' about our approach.

Training for Baghdad in northern Australia was problematic. We drove armoured vehicles fast around the barracks in the middle of the night, practising our formations and trying to replicate scenarios we might encounter; we sat on rooftops in the rain to replicate what it might be like if an angry mob attacked us; we got sprayed with capsicum spray so we would understand its effect if we ever needed to use it; we watched videos of insurgents beheading kidnap victims in an effort to understand the environment and the people; we turned Darwin into Baghdad and trained like we were there.

The rest of the army did a lot to support us. During parts of the training, hundreds of soldiers role-played local Iraqis, foreign military and embassy officials. Occasionally you'd get a wink from a 'local Iraqi' truck driver you recognised.

The army bought new equipment, including spending millions of dollars on remote-controlled machine-gun mounts. These mounts had a thumb-operated controller, just like on a video-game console. From the crew commander's cupola (the small hatch that opens next to the engine deck), you watched a screen at thigh level as you spun the gun quickly onto targets. These mounts were highly accurate, but very difficult to master. They had been purchased after the blokes already in Iraq complained the vehicle set-up had the crew commander standing behind the .50 calibre machine gun while the vehicle was in motion. This meant he was driving through the streets of Baghdad almost totally exposed – 'balls up'.

With the new remote system, the commander could crouch in his cupola and operate the gun. But what the new design and technology didn't take into account was that a lot of the time you really needed to be standing out the top of the vehicle – directing traffic out of the way, or showing your pistol to stop drivers cutting you off. You couldn't do that from within the vehicle. We did scratch our heads a little as to why the government insisted on spending millions on these systems, but it was new, shiny technology, and we were happy to accept it.

We were also trained to use automatic grenade launchers, until then only used by Special Forces. These fit on the remote system and were thought to be useful as counter-ambush weapons in the open areas up in northern Iraq. A Special Air Service Regiment warrant officer instructed us on how to operate them: how to reload, how to fix stoppages, and how to use the tool for getting out a grenade wedged in the barrel after firing too many rounds. We learnt all this without knowing whether we could actually fire the weapon, as the only ammunition we could get was 'environmentally stressed' – apparently it had been sitting in a shipping container in the Kuwaiti sun for a year.

The Chief of Army, Lieutenant General Peter Leahy, had to sign off personally before we could fire these rounds. He came to view our training just after we had been through a particularly rigorous period, during which I had slept a handful of hours over a few days. I was tired and pissed off as he instructed me on the precautions my troop needed to take before we could fire the ammunition. He directed that everyone had to wear body armour and ballistic goggles, and everyone not firing should be behind cover in an armoured vehicle or in a bunker. He started lecturing me, quite rightly, on all of this.

When he started talking about the danger of a grenade being caught in the barrel, I disagreed with him on some point and said something arrogant like, 'No, sir, that is a known design feature of the weapon and we have been trained how to fix the stoppage.'

I saw my commanding officer behind him grimace.

General Leahy looked at me and said, 'If you don't follow all these safety precautions, firstly I'll sack you' – he turned to point at my brigade commander, John Cantwell, standing just to his right – 'and then I'll sack him.'

I was shocked. I suddenly realised how concerned General Leahy was about using this stressed ammunition and that I should shut my mouth. I politely agreed to do everything he said, then left, resolving not to upset generals and jeopardise brigadiers' careers.

Through these months of training, we were also trying to spend time with our families and lead normal lives. I was in charge of twenty-seven blokes, which generated a lot of administration:

deployment order details, wills in case the worst occurred, power-of-attorney forms, official passport applications, immunisations, dog tags – all needed to be checked and re-checked.

I attended my sergeant's wedding, held social functions with my troop, said goodbye to family who visited me in Darwin before I left, wrote letters to my troop's next of kin telling them as much as I could, and made a clumsy proposal to my girlfriend. By the time we were ready to go, I was tired of training, happy to be engaged and ready to get on with the job.

*

Crystal and I had been together only a year when I left for Baghdad the first time.

We had a classic romance. Love at first sight. She moved from the Gold Coast to Darwin after knowing me for only a matter of weeks. We just knew it was right, from the first night we met. Her airy, giggly way added a vibrancy to my life I had never known.

We loved spending all our free time together. We'd go out dancing in the bars on Mitchell Street, or talk till all hours of the night, or just lie on the couch watching movies. I loved everything about her. She had a way of disarming people and getting them to like her. Under an unassuming demeanour, she was a talented theatre nurse who received praise from even the most indifferent surgeons. She vacuumed the house in a bikini, laughed at all my stupid jokes, and, to my surprise and good fortune, was just as in love with me as I was with her.

During our first year together, we watched other lieutenants deploy to Iraq, and Crystal knew I would probably go too at some stage. She also knew how much I wanted to go. Maybe I was naive, but like all my peers I was desperate to do the job for real. She knew how much it meant to me.

Crystal did a good job of keeping it together, but when I left her at the airport she went home miserable. She planned to stay at home for a few weeks before travelling to London to see friends. This holiday would be her way of passing time while we were apart. I was travelling and having adventures, so why shouldn't she? Friends were coming to mind the house and look after my dog while we were away.

The day I left, Crystal sat on the steps of our house in Darwin crying, worried about my safety and uncertain how she would cope with our being apart for four months. It was then that my old dog, Girlie, a Labrador–Kelpie cross, did something strange.

I had had Girlie since I was in high school. She had followed me around the country and had witnessed so much of my life. She must have moved house twenty times or more throughout her life. As Crystal sat on the stairs, Girlie sat next to her and leaned back on her hind legs, putting both paws up on Crystal's shoulders, something I had never known her to do before. It was as if she were giving Crystal a hug.

I had always felt that Girlie was very in tune with people's emotions, but perhaps this was more than that. Some might claim that Girlie had a sixth sense. Perhaps she knew something was going to happen. Perhaps she was trying to tell Crystal that I was going to get hurt, but not to worry because in the end it would be OK.

Or maybe Girlie just hadn't been walked in a few days. Poor neglected mutt.

2

TO IRAQ

WE WENT TO WAR LIKE SO MANY SOLDIERS of my generation – by commercial air travel.

My introduction to the Middle East was a ten-hour stopover in the Emirates business lounge at Dubai International. Nervous about what lay ahead, I passed the hours on the leather couches in glass smoking rooms, puffing through an endless chain of cigarettes and watching the waves of travellers go by.

The wide marble halls and cavernous domed ceilings of the airport were not what I had expected. The high-end boutiques, the elegant women in tailored full black-silk niqabs, swaying their hips as they walked to their departure gates, the shiny dark-skinned men with their matching shiny jewellery and sweat-stained shirts – no-one had explained this was part of going to Iraq.

I was in a group of about twenty officers and senior soldiers, an advance party who would commence the handover with our counterparts in Baghdad before our ninety companions arrived.

We sat around awkwardly in our shorts and collared shirts, with recently cropped hair, trying to look inconspicuous. Our camouflage backpacks didn't help.

A short flight to Kuwait International and we were getting closer. Sweltering heat and steamy dirty hallways with green lino floors, dotted with surly guards; being herded through baggage claim and immigration with badly photocopied letters of introduction that somehow made our arrival without visas legitimate; the hour-and-a-half wait for lost baggage to be found – it wasn't war, but I was already on edge.

Then followed a few days in the sweltering Kuwaiti heat doing final training before heading into Iraq. We drove in coaches out to rifle ranges pegged out of patches of desert. The heat was intense. One of the older warrant officers passed out, having been off the air-conditioned bus no longer than five minutes. As we helped him back onto the bus, I wondered how we would be able to work in this climate. Our body armour and helmets seemed to trap the heat and keep us constantly moist with sweat.

We were introduced to a new bandage that set hard when it came in contact with blood. It was designed to save your life if your arm or leg was torn off in a bomb blast – they called this explosive amputation. Apparently, since the first improvised explosive devices (IEDs) emerged mid-way through the previous year, it had become a common way for soldiers to die. IEDs had quickly become the insurgents' weapons of choice. So you needed a bandage that would solidify quickly over your bloodied stump before you died of blood loss. We had to sign a consent form, because it was not approved for use in Australia – apparently the doctors had to do a lot of damage to get the solid bandage off once you made it to hospital.

We got our new bandages and confirmed which pocket to put them in so whoever was giving you first aid knew where to look. We were issued with a last round of equipment: new helmets, cold weather gear, including sub-zero puffer jackets (which seemed ridiculous at the time, but we were to be in northern Iraq during winter), a fifth set of fire-retardant gloves.

Finally, the day came when we got on the C-130 Hercules. The flight was painful: we wore all our protective equipment, and the seating in the plane – aluminium poles slung with fabric straps – was cramped and hot. As we approached Baghdad, the pilot started manoeuvring in a way designed either to piss us off or to avoid surface-to-air fire. Maybe both. Shooting at planes was a regular pastime for the insurgents. They'd sit just off the perimeter of the airfield and take pot shots at the landing aircraft. I swore as sharp pains jabbed through my ears from the changes in air pressure as the aircraft banked, turned and dropped sharply into Baghdad International Airport.

*

Baghdad – flat, hot, congested, a city of seven million situated along a series of bends in the Tigris River. In the region known as the 'cradle of civilisation', it lies just 80 kilometres north of the ancient biblical city of Babylon. But I don't recall the Bible mentioning anything about Australians in armoured vehicles.

On arrival we were picked up from the airport by a patrol of blokes who were about to hand over to us at SECDET.

I quickly learnt about one of the habits you had to adopt when moving through Baghdad with your head up in an armoured vehicle. The leaking sewers that kept the median strips green also left large puddles of shit water across the road. The veteran crew I was with knew to duck their heads, but I wanted to take in as much of this new city as possible from my position in the front crew hatch. I watched the vehicle hit a puddle of raw sewage

Streets of Baghdad with overflowing sewage.

and, without time to react, was covered in a bow wave that went straight in my mouth and left me dry-retching at regular intervals throughout the day.

The road from the airport forked as it approached the Tigris. Crossing over the river to the east took you towards the Karadah Peninsula and our accommodation, known as 'the Flats'. Heading north-east led you into the International Zone, or Green Zone as it was sometimes called.

The Flats, a ten-storey building, was an obvious landmark in a city that was relatively low-rise. It was surrounded by dusty weather-beaten hotels and an old hospital. Nearby, on the same long stretch of land, was the University of Baghdad, with a fairly extensive campus that took up several square kilometres.

The Flats was the hub of all our activities – our accommodation, kitchen and dining hall, command post, vehicle parking and servicing area. Most importantly, it was the backbone of the defences, not just for ourselves, but also the Australian embassy, which was next door. For twenty-four hours a day we had infantry manning machine guns at each corner, covering all approaches to our building and the embassy. The snipers sat on the roof, day in, day out, covering our movements and watching for anything out of the ordinary.

My first couple of days at the Flats were a blur of activity. The handover from the outgoing troop leader involved meeting the embassy staff, familiarising myself with the building defence and routine, understanding the condition of the vehicles, and

The Flats.

starting to get to know this strange new city we would be working in. Even just finding my way around the Flats at times got me unstuck – there were so many dark corridors that looked the same.

I had a bed allocated in a room with two other officers, but during those first few days I only saw it for the few seconds before my head, which was spinning, hit the pillow.

As in most parts of the city, the sewage system leaked regularly and the electricity was intermittent due to an over-extended power grid. From the sentry position on the fourth floor, you could hear the air conditioners thump on, then off, as you looked out on the green grassy median strips and trees that lined the roads.

The Flats itself had obviously been designed to be one of the more opulent buildings in Baghdad. At times I would imagine how it would have looked had it ever been completed. From the outside, the building would have oozed wealth, with its sandstone façades and high windows that gave it a classical but also unmistakably Middle Eastern look. The large entranceway that opened onto the four-lane road at the front would have had arched doors of highly polished metal and glass. Entering through these doors, you would have found a large, cool, open expanse. I imagined white tiles across the lobby and a glass elevator that rode up the centre of the cylindrical building, all the way to the tenth floor. The rooms, whether hotel rooms or apartments, would be cool and chic, with the well-appointed bathrooms and kitchen overdone and tacky in the style of many of Baghdad's high-end buildings.

The tenth floor, I envisaged, would have been either a restaurant or an extremely large penthouse for only the wealthiest visitors or tenants. The large archways on two of the four sides would be set with glass to give one of the best views over Baghdad, a city that I came to find strangely beautiful.

However, construction on the Flats had stopped after the basic structure had been completed. A few rooms had been tiled, but on the whole the building was a shell. There were no windows or doors: only what the Australian occupants had put in place by way of plywood sheets that used a unique self-closing mechanism, fashioned using water-bottle weights and a rudimentary pulley system.

When I first arrived, I couldn't help but think of the movie *Mad Max Beyond Thunderdome*. The interior of the building, an open cylindrical area about 7 metres in diameter, made the rest of the dark, gaping doorway and scaffolding seem to loom over my head. The makeshift elevator that groaned up to the tenth floor only added to the feeling that at any minute two opponents would swing into the open expanse and attempt to sever each other's limbs with chainsaws.

I didn't know for sure why the Flats had not been completed, but the rumour was that during the building process the owner had become aware that one of Saddam's sons was interested in acquiring it (by dubious, most likely illegal and possibly violent means). To forestall this, the owner had just stopped building. In the long term he may even have done all right from the venture, as the Australian government was paying exorbitant rent for use of the half-completed structure.

The building was poorly lit, and only the first couple of floors were occupied. Many areas were mazes of dusty concrete walls and dark corners. Despite all this, since the arrival of the first security detachment in early 2003, the Australians had done a good job of making it home. They had sandbagged up the open windows for protection and furnished the rooms they were allocated with pictures of home or pages from men's magazines. As time passed, heaters were put in for the cold winters, and air conditioners were fitted to make the scorching summers bearable. Army stretchers were replaced with beds, and deals were struck with the US military to supply bulk rations; a kitchen opened on the first floor, ending the need to live on ration packs.

The focal point of the building was the Australian flag that flew in the open expanse that ran up through the centre of the building.

Open shaft at the centre of the Flats.

Around us, Baghdad's low-rise central business district slowly melted into urban sprawl, then thinned into rural areas on the outskirts. The Tigris was the lifeblood of the city. Tracks of green palms and grass extended on either side of the river, out as far as the water would reach. After this, there was desert: undulating hills of dirt and sand.

The city was scattered with palaces: Saddam's legacy. These were usually poorly built sandstone façades on steel frames. The façades had limited life spans in the harsh conditions. The war had blown many of the sandstone panels off to reveal the frames underneath, like rips and tears in the leathered skin of a dead animal left to rot in the desert sun. Rockets had left gaping holes in other buildings.

Several of these large palaces were just to the east of the airport, and about 12 kilometres from the Flats. This whole area had been taken over by the Coalition forces and turned into a set of mini-cities: Camp Victory, Camp Stryker, Camp Liberty and Camp Slayer. Each was a jumble of palaces, demountable buildings and tents.

Al-Faw Palace, the largest one of all, situated in Camp Victory, was the headquarters of the occupying forces. Next door, about 300 metres away, was the Australian headquarters, occupying a smaller building, all tacky marble and gold fittings. These palaces had been built on the banks of an artificial lake that Hussein had had excavated and filled with fish. Small hills in nearby Camp Slayer were formed from the spoils of the excavation. The hills made good aiming marks for insurgents firing rockets into the base.

The interior of the palace used by the Australians had been partitioned into office areas, using plywood and folding tables. All Australian operations in the Middle East were run out of here, under the command of a brigadier, or equivalent from the navy or air force. I would come here often in the months ahead.

Large, solid, wooden double doors opened from the Australian headquarters onto a roadway that ran around the lake and joined the maze of roads running through Camp Victory, linking it to the other camps. The way to Camp Slayer was via a tunnel that our armoured vehicles only just fit through. With the antenna folded down, you could drive through it and run your hand along the ceiling.

Near the Slayer tunnel was the main entrance to the whole base complex, a series of chicanes to slow traffic, concrete barriers, machine-gun towers and boom gates that led onto Route Irish. This was, at the time, arguably the most dangerous road in the world, due to the sporadic sniper fire and constant threat of improvised explosive device (IED) or roadside bomb attacks. It was the main route for Coalition forces travelling to and from the airport. For anyone keen to try their hand at attacking a Coalition convoy, it must have been like shooting fish in a barrel.

3

FIRST TASK

OUR VEHICLE, THE AUSTRALIAN LIGHT Armoured Vehicle, or ASLAV, was a workhorse, and a real source of pride for the cavalry soldiers. The first ASLAVs were bought in the early 1990s as medium-range reconnaissance vehicles. Some of them carried the formidable 25-mm chain gun in a two-man turret, and there was also a personnel-carrying variant with room in the back for nine at a squeeze.

The ASLAV was the obvious choice for Baghdad. It had eight wheels, all with run-flat tyres – so it was fast. It could sit on 110 kilometres per hour without a problem and keep up with traffic on the highways. The chain gun could elevate to fire at insurgents shooting from high-rises, and the two-man turret could quickly traverse 360° to cover the rear of the vehicle just as well as the front.

The personnel-carrying variant was used for transporting lower-ranking embassy staff or military people, while the ambassador preferred to travel in his armoured BMW. When escorting the ambassador, we usually positioned an ASLAV with a .50 calibre forward. The .50 calibre was a great gun, but quite unwieldy and inaccurate. An ASLAV with the 25-mm chain gun would be at the rear. The ambassador's car would be wedged between the two and driven by the military police close personal protection team.

A few months before my arrival in Iraq, the BMW had been crunched by the rear ASLAV in heavy traffic. The ambassador, who had been in the job since the invasion in 2003 and who was not shy about expressing his views, was not happy about this, and the boys heard all about it.

*

The model governing our introduction to Iraq, in fact the whole tour, invovled staggering duties as much as possible. New blokes would always be paired with teams who had been there for a while. Individuals would be scattered among experienced crews, or else a new vehicle crew would form part of a patrol with experienced teams. Even SECDET rotations were staggered, with troops rotating in and out every two months. Generally we kept with the teams that we had trained with back in Australia, but some individuals and crews would come earlier or leave later.

This meant that new teams weren't all on their own and in danger of getting lost – Baghdad in 2004 was not a city you wanted to get lost in. Driving the streets in 13-tonne armoured vehicles, we stood out as obvious targets for insurgents. We made a lot of noise: the exhaust fans of the supercharged Detroit diesel engines shrieked as we accelerated, and the Jacobs (engine compression) brake howled as we braked hard into corners. We sat above the traffic, many of us with our upper bodies exposed, protected only by our gloves, goggles and body armour.

My first proper task was to drive to Balad, about an hour north of Baghdad, to meet the remaining half of my troop. They were flying into Balad direct from Australia with three new vehicles to replace ones that had been in Iraq for a year already and were now in need of a complete overhaul.

Balad, named Logistics Support Area Anaconda by the US military, was the central logistics hub for the Americans. Everything came and went into the country through it, a city built from tents and demountables around an old Iraqi airfield.

One of the sergeants who had been in the country for four months was put in charge of the patrol to Balad. While I was of a higher rank, he had the experience, and I was happy for him to command the patrol so that I could get my head around this new environment.

In 2004 Baghdad was functioning like any other city. There were traffic jams, pedestrians, red lights, sidewalk restaurants, street vendors, markets and streets of shopfronts. It was a densely populated city, and most of its inhabitants were just trying to get on with life. At the same time, they had to deal with the complexities of life in a war zone. Paul Bremer's 'de-Ba'athification' of the ruling class – the removal of all of Saddam's former Ba'ath Party influences from the new government, which resulted in the dismissal of an estimated 50,000 former regime-affiliated government employees, including military and police – left massive gaps in the country's ability to look after its people. The army and police were left with poor leadership, and many once-proud officers had turned to the insurgency and were now fighting to destabilise the country and thus prove that they were needed and the Americans were not.

Intelligence reports said Baghdad had up to 40,000 active insurgents. While the Kurds and their armed fighters, the Peshmerga, generally looked after their own, the Sunnis and Shias fought because they saw they had so much to lose; they vied for power and influence in the vacuum left by Saddam's demise. They fought not only against the American-led forces, but also with each other. Kidnappings had become common, followed by reports of headless corpses floating in the Tigris. Bombs were going off in predominantly Shia neighbourhoods, in marketplaces, mosques, outdoor restaurants and cafes. Sunnis would claim responsibility and Shias would retaliate. At any given time, you could stand on the roof of the Flats and watch smoke rise from far-off parts of the city. An explosion might be heard from a leafy neighbourhood not far from the banks of the Tigris; a busy intersection would erupt as a Sunni suicide bomber targeted a busload of Shia schoolchildren or a military patrol; rockets would crack and fizz from Sadr City and thump into the International Zone. There was always something, and anytime you listened it seemed you could pick up the sound of a siren echoing somewhere in the city.

This was the city we snaked our patrol through, along the congested streets to link up with Highway 1, which ran the length of the country from north to south. This road took us to Balad.

The thinking was that you had to make yourself a hard target: make any insurgent think twice about attacking. We drove with safety catches off – the 25-mm chain gun ready to fire, the machine guns cocked and ready to go in the event that we identified a suicide bomber trying to swerve into one of our vehicles.

We careered through traffic, driving at more than 100 kilometres an hour through the city streets, trying to minimise the time any insurgent might have to shoot at us or detonate a bomb as we drove past. We ran red lights – straight through. We nudged cars out of the way, even on the highway when they were doing 100 kilometres an hour themselves. If they looked like they might be trying to slow us, we would give them a tap. Sometimes they would be knocked onto the other side of the road, into oncoming traffic, sometimes they would brake hard and spin to face back the way they had come, and sometimes they would swerve off the road and down an embankment in a cloud of dust. We didn't stop – we couldn't. This was how we operated in Baghdad, where patrols and convoys like ours were getting blown up every day.

Did we make the city safer? Did we ever prevent a suicide IED attack? Probably not, but we were there to do a specific job, which was to protect the embassy staff and allow them to do their diplomatic work. Getting ourselves blown up, or shot, or caught in a complex ambush with insurgents peppering our vehicle with machine-gun fire while IEDs exploded under us wouldn't achieve that. We weren't there to make Iraq safer or to defeat the insurgency.

Was I comfortable with the aggressive way we drove? To be honest, I wasn't. I was really taken aback by those first patrols in Baghdad and Balad. But I was working alongside blokes who had been there for four months, which may not seem like much, but they had been through a lot in that time. Many had witnessed a large truck being driven through the gates of the base up north and detonated in front of the dining hall. The place had been almost levelled by the explosion, and US and Iraqi soldiers, plus contracted workers from the Philippines and Bangladesh, had been killed. It had occurred only forty-five minutes after the Australian commander had been eating in that same mess hall. And that was just one incident.

These blokes had seen a large vehicle-borne IED detonate out the front of the Flats. They had seen the blood smear on the footpath from a young boy who helped his family run the small roadside stall there: it had been obliterated when the IED detonated. From the Flats they had witnessed with their own eyes his father's grief.

They had been involved in a horrific high-speed accident where an ASLAV had flipped end over end after hitting a mound of dirt on the side of the road at speed. A colleague of mine, my old squadron sergeant major back in the cavalry regiment, had been in the back of the vehicle. When the American soldiers came to assist, they opened the back and assumed he was dead, as the large steel fridge had broken free and scalped him as the vehicle flipped. It was only later, when they heard him moaning, that they realised he was still alive. He made a full recovery.

They had been through so many rocket attacks and been roused from their sleep by so many random explosions that they were on edge. I couldn't blame them for driving the way they did. I definitely couldn't get them to slow down, or tone down their aggressive driving, until all their commanders had rotated out. So it was later, when the handover was complete, that I spoke to my blokes and told them that, yes, we were driving too fast, and yes, we were too aggressive. I felt that we were missing the point of what was trying to be achieved in Iraq and that the way we were acting was playing its own small part in adding to the instability of the country. I also felt that we were putting ourselves at far greater risk of injury from high-speed vehicle accidents than from anything the insurgents could do to us.

Later events may have proved this wrong, but I stand by what I said. I even reprimanded a soldier for hitting a civilian vehicle for no obvious good reason and moved him so that he no longer drove an armoured vehicle but was a shooter in the rear hatch. This bloke had been there for two months longer than me and he was pissed off with my decision – but I was comfortable it was right, and my troop sergeant did a good job backing me up.

What so much of this came down to was that there were many people in this country who wanted to kill us – and a far greater number didn't give two shits whether we lived or died. This is something that as Australians we had never been exposed to. In Australia, homicidal people are few and far between, and most are identified and locked away. Not in Baghdad. They lived in huge numbers among the population, actively looking for our vulnerabilities, or rather, for any way at all to attack Coalition forces. If they had their chance, they would drag our bodies through the streets and relish their victory over their country's invaders.

I don't think that I truly understood this in 2004. I also believe that those soldiers who did grasp this were the ones who didn't fare so well when they returned to Australia.

Our route took us through Baghdad, out into the rural area to the north of the city and west of the Tigris. It seemed the only place you would see women in niqabs was in the rural areas; in Baghdad the women were a lot less traditional in their dress. Many wore jeans and scarves that covered their hair, but not their faces. Most younger women were well groomed and used make-up. So I was surprised to see small, dark niqab-clad figures working with the men in the fields in the hot sun: I had assumed that women working the land in scorching heat would be more likely to have a relaxed dress code than women who lived in the city, but this was not the case.

When we turned off the highway, we were met with a series of signs in both English and Arabic. These were the same signs that you saw all over the country as you approached US military checkpoints.

STOP

Show ID

You are approaching a Military Checkpoint.

And then we saw:

Welcome to LSA Anaconda

Queues of Iraqis in cars were waiting to have their IDs checked so they could enter the base. Thousands of locals came to provide services to the soldiers. They would run small shops, sell trinkets or give haircuts. They would work as cleaners, collect garbage, act as interpreters, or acquire and sell local produce, including vegetables, to bolster the freeze-dried, bulk-packed rations that had come from the US or been flown in from elsewhere in the Middle East. The locals employed on the base all made good money, significantly more than they could make in the local markets. That was why they risked sitting in the queues out the front of the base.

A checkpoint onto a base was one of the most dangerous places you could ever be. There was a chance you would be shot by a nervous soldier who mistook you reaching for your ID as an attempt to trigger a suicide switch that would blow you both to Allah. Or you might become collateral damage as a real suicide bomber detonated his deadly payload when the guards approached his vehicle.

But we drove past the queue without incident, down the lane marked 'Military Vehicles Only'. A quick flash of an ID and we were through the gate and onto the base.

The size of Balad was astounding, especially as it had only been built in the last twelve months. Now it was home to over 35,000 US soldiers. We heard reports from the Americans that the base had the same social issues you get in any large population centre, particularly one where the vast majority of the population is aged between twenty and thirty-five. There was rape, drug use, murder and gang violence. There were areas where you were advised not to go after dark, bars (with alcohol-free beer) and salsa-dancing nights. And there was also the occasional rocket strike. The farmland that ringed the base made it easy for insurgents to fire rockets and escape before they could be found by an attack helicopter, which would be up and scouring the area within a couple of minutes of each attack.

Because the population of soldiers was so densely packed in such a small area, and because the insurgents would aim for the dining halls at mealtimes, injuries were common. A female soldier had been killed the day before we arrived.

We drove onto the base and went looking for a refuelling station to top up our vehicles. When we rounded the last of a vast row of green and tan air-conditioned tents, the view was awe-inspiring. Helicopters lined the airfield from one end to the other, hundreds of them sitting in the dusty shimmering heat: Black Hawks, SuperCobras, Apaches and Chinooks. Then behind them were rows of transport planes, the workhorses that flew in and out of the country, bringing supplies from Kuwait, Diego Garcia and mainland USA, and taking casualties out to Germany and body bags back home to the US. The airfield was constantly rumbling with something coming or leaving.

After refuelling we found the garrison commander's office, called the 'sheriff's office', and were allocated our tents. Each one slept about twenty people in bunk beds. We cleaned our guns and checked over the vehicles. We tried to raise headquarters using the satellite radio, but quickly realised that no-one really knew how to use the unit, nor its strange directional antenna that looked like a small upside-down Hills Hoist clothes line. So we just called them on the satellite phone. We found the 'dining facility' and had some dinner. Walking back to the vehicles, the sergeant who was with us would greet passing US soldiers in his broadest Australian drawl: 'G'day, mate. How're ya bum grubs?' They'd reply, 'Yes sir, good, thank you, sir, have a nice day.' Who says Australian isn't a dialect?

We went to the PX (post exchange, the store on US bases) to get some near-beer (non-alcoholic beer) that we jammed into the air-conditioning vent to keep cold. Then we slowly wound down for the evening.

The next day, the new vehicles from Australia arrived with the remainder of my troop. The boys were excited to be in Iraq and, it seemed, just as excited that they had been allowed to smoke in the transport aircraft while it was in the air. It sounded as though they had spent most of their time cracking jokes, smoking and winding each other up during the long flight from Darwin to Diego Garcia, smack-bang in the middle of the Indian Ocean, then through to Balad.

We rolled the new vehicles out through the lifted nose of the plane and drove them to the vehicle park near our tents to prep them for the drive back to Baghdad. Even after all the promises that the vehicles would arrive with ammunition, I wasn't really surprised that they had arrived with none. I left my troop sergeant to look after our vehicles and went in search of some rounds. After wandering through the maze of demountable office buildings, I came across the quartermaster's store and a young corporal. It sounded like getting 7.62 mm and .50 calibre rounds for our machine guns wouldn't be a problem. But I got a quizzical look when I asked about 25-mm ammunition for the chain gun. After explaining that we had the same guns in our vehicles as the 25-mm gun of the US Bradleys, the corporal finally clicked: 'Oh, you need 25 mike mike.'

These 25-mm rounds come in several 'natures', namely high-explosive and armour-piercing. The high-explosive round has a small charge that detonates on impact. The armour-piercing round has a steel dart that, when fired, is carried out of the barrel in a plastic case called a sabot. As it leaves the end of the barrel, the sabot breaks away and the dart, or slug, punches through pretty much anything in its way. The armour-piercing ammunition used by Australia has a tungsten dart, whereas the US equivalent uses a slightly denser, depleted-uranium dart, referred to as 'DU'.

So when this young corporal asked what kind of 25 mike mike rounds I wanted, I thought I would try my luck and replied, 'DU.' At which point he realised he didn't have the authority to issue depleted-uranium rounds, so he went to find his boss to get permission. We had obviously pushed too far, as his boss asked us a hundred questions and we left with nothing, not a single round. It was probably for the better that we didn't get any DU – there would have been questions . . . possibly followed by medical testing. There was a lot of controversy around whether the depleted uranium was carcinogenic.

We ended up splitting the ammunition from the older vehicles and returned to Baghdad with only a half ammunition load for each vehicle – more than enough, even if we got into a shitfight.

Fortunately we didn't. I returned to the Flats that night with a full troop and three new vehicles. I had been in Iraq for four days.

4

DAY-TO-DAY BAGHDAD

WE QUICKLY GOT USED TO DRIVING IN BAGHDAD and working hard to present a hard target. We would have the 25-mm cannon traversing, in constant motion, shifting its point of aim to the spot we considered the most dangerous. As we drove, my gunner and I had our heads up out of the turret. We did this for several reasons. First, moving at speed through a built-up area made looking through a vehicle sight, or periscope, useless, as all you saw were blurred images as you sped by. Second, locals reacted to eye contact. The fastest way to determine a driver's intention as he approached was to point a 25-mm cannon towards him and look him in the eye – it would instantly become clear whether he was a suicide IED driver or merely a commuter attempting to try his luck passing a Coalition convoy. We also used our pistols a lot in traffic, for similar reasons. Crew commanders would pull their pistol and point it at a driver – the look in the driver's eye would always let you know what they were thinking.

Pistols were particularly effective in managing traffic. One explanation I heard for this was that the locals (and possible insurgents) understood that if I fired a 25-mm cannon at them, they would likely die and go to Allah, but if I fired a pistol, it was unlikely to kill and would probably cause them a lot of pain. I was also told that a pistol carried a lot of intimidation value because Saddam's henchmen had used them in acts of extreme violence against the civilian population.

The way we drove those dusty roads was manic. We thundered down the highways with the turrets spinning from one side to the other, slewing the vehicles from one lane to another as we passed under bridges and overpasses. Insurgents had taken to dropping grenades on convoys as they emerged on the far side of an overpass, but changing lanes underneath meant we left them guessing where we would appear. We would emerge with the turrets pointing backwards to where any attacker would be waiting, the 25-mm ready to blow him to pieces.

We also had shooters up with light machine guns on their shoulders. We were always ready for something to happen, always presenting a hard target – poised to unleash a maelstrom of supersonic high-explosive rounds and machine-gun bullets. The idea was to make any insurgent think twice about attacking us.

*

Since the first IED strikes on US soldiers in mid-2003, the insurgents had been learning from their successes and failures, targeting both Coalition troops and Iraqi security forces. We said, even back then, that there were only clever IED makers left, as the stupid ones had blown themselves up long ago.

The IEDs were getting more and more sophisticated. Radio-controlled switches, using remote-control garage-door technology or remote-control toy parts, were common. These were used to complete the circuit that would send a current from the battery pack to the detonator, which would explode, igniting the main charge – an explosive reaction that could blast air and fragments at up to 8000 metres per second and instantaneously create over-pressure in the confined space of an armoured vehicle, which could break down the cellular structure of tissue in the human lungs and brain. After IED strikes, armoured crewmen were regularly found dead without a scratch on them, their brains and lungs a mash.

The succession of wars fought in Iraq had left a supply of munitions, referred to as 'explosive remnants of war', that could be easily adapted for use as main charges. Artillery rounds, mortar bombs, grenades and rockets were the most common. There were stories of the Americans and Iraqis alike abandoning huge stockpiles of munitions. So the insurgents had an ample supply of explosives.

And when we found ways to jam the radio-controlled switches, they would just change back to a 'command wire' switch. In this case, the bomb was detonated by a triggerman in a concealed location who would physically press a button, or, even more crudely, join two bare wires, thus completing a circuit. The current would run from a battery pack down the wire to the explosives. While this technique had its limitations, with the triggerman having to be within 100 metres of the bomb, it was still a very effective way of targeting conveys.

There was talk of the insurgents using Russian anti-armour charges, which would explosively fire ball bearings that could penetrate the hull of a vehicle, particularly the light armour of our ASLAVs. The insurgents were constantly looking for new ways to defeat whatever we tried to do to protect ourselves.

Then there were the suicide bombers. What can you do to protect yourself against someone who has decided to die in order to take you with him? We would get daily threat reports from the intelligence blokes: 'Look out for a yellow taxi with mixed panels, sagging on its suspension, driven by a male between 20 and 40 years of age, cleanly shaven and sweating' – which came close to describing a third of the cars on the road. There were heaps of yellow taxis with shitty panel-beating jobs. They all sagged on their suspensions, whether they had bombs in the back or not. As for 20- to 40-year-olds, cleanly shaven and sweating: most men in Baghdad didn't wear beards and it was fucking hot, so they sweated – probably about as much as if they were about to blow themselves to Allah.

There was always talk of snipers, and a lot of the boys thought they had been fired on at one time or another, particularly on Route Irish. On one occasion, a patrol commander came back swearing that he had been shot at and showed us the indent in the smoke-grenade discharger on the side of his turret. Something didn't smell quite right, and this commander had been known to fire off his pistol as he drove down Route Irish. We looked at the angle of the indent. It was all wrong for sniper fire; it was the perfect size of a 9-mm round – the same as our Browning pistols. He must have shot his own smoke-grenade discharger with his pistol. He was about to rotate back to Australia, so we let it slide. But it left a bad taste in our mouths to think that our blokes could be driving around firing off rounds with such careless neglect that they could strike their own vehicle – what else were they inadvertently hitting?

Then there were the rockets. These were not necessarily a daily event – at least not the ones that landed anywhere near us – but there was always the threat that a rocket could hit at any moment.

The Flats had some pretty crude toilets. The urinal on the accommodation level on the eastern side of the building had a sandbagged wall where the window should have been. The sandbags only went up a couple of metres, so there was a large gap between the sandbags and the ceiling. There was a step so you could overlook the four-lane road that ran east. A few restaurants and cafes lined the road out that way. Lots of locals still went to these restaurants, trying to carry on with their lives in defiance of the war.

The little room had a porcelain urinal bolted to the wall and plumbed in – a touch of luxury. The first time a rocket hit near us, I was using this urinal. The rocket struck in front of a building about 70 metres east of the Flats, one of the restaurants that would have been full of people had it been a few hours later, in the early evening. Because the 'bathroom' had a gap between the sandbags and the ceiling, the percussion from the blast thumped through into the room. Dust kicked up everywhere and I was unceremoniously thrown off balance, spraying piss on the wall and a little on my boots.

*

Not too long after this, the Chief of the Defence Force, General Peter Cosgrove, visited, and it made for a surreal day. Beforehand, we had a walk-in, a local who approached the front gate of the Flats to warn us of an attack planned for that night. He told us that about twenty insurgents armed with machine guns and rocket-propelled grenades intended to attack our building at 0100 hours that night. He claimed he had just come from a meeting with the insurgents, who were finalising their plans.

A few things didn't add up about this local, but we took the threat very seriously, particularly as the general was visiting. We did our own planning and decided it would be best to move him and the embassy staff into Camp Victory for the night.

Just as night was falling over the city, I briefed General Cosgrove and his security team on our planed route and 'actions-on' in the event of an incident. In the twilight, he nodded along as I briefed; he didn't ask any questions and seemed comfortable with the plan. He was then directed to one of the personnel carriers, and the embassy staff were loaded into a second. Just on last light,

I gave the word over the radio, and the first vehicle of the four-car patrol started to roll. As it snaked out of the checkpoint at the front of the Flats, it hit a spot of sodden soil from the ever-leaking sewage. The engine revved, the wheels spun and it slid back into the mud.

I heard the call from one of the other crew commanders – 'Give 'em a kiss' – and the second vehicle rolled forward and nudged the bogged car. The bump knocked it up and out of the muddy patch and the convoy was off down the road.

We had moved through the International Zone and past the old Ba'ath Party headquarters when a message was passed from one of the embassy staff through to the military police security team to the vehicle crew, who in turn relayed it to me: 'Can you slow down, because it's a bit bumpy?' It took me a minute to take in that one of the embassy staff was complaining about a bumpy ride – did she know where she was? After a minute I replied, 'We are travelling down one of the most dangerous roads in the world at one of the most dangerous times of night. My primary concern is their safety, not their comfort.' I don't think the message was passed on.

After we returned from Camp Victory, having dropped off the general and the ambassador and his staff, we returned to the Flats without incident. We all sat around at 0100 in the morning, helmets and body armour on, crews in their vehicles waiting to react. The minutes ticked by so slowly. Nothing occurred.

*

I was so busy I didn't have much time to call Crystal. But I thought about her all the time. We were planning on holding an engagement party once I returned.

Even when she was travelling in the UK and Europe, I could speak to her on her mobile. I usually called in the middle of the night after I'd finished my night-time shift at the command post. For security reasons, I couldn't talk about much, so she would tell me about what she had been up to. It was a little piece of normality in this strange world.

5

US AND THEM

ALTHOUGH I HAD CREWS FOR THREE PATROLS, I tried to get out on the road myself at least once a day. There were many reasons for this: so I could show the blokes I was not some snot-nosed officer who spent his days in the air-conditioned command post; so I could give one of my crew commanders a short break; so I could keep in touch with the environment my troop worked in all day; so I could keep an eye on my blokes; and, to be honest, because it was exciting and I was a young lieutenant working in Baghdad with the opportunity to get out on the road – so why wouldn't I?

I would walk into the Australian headquarters at Camp Victory, face and uniform covered in grime from the road and the exhaust, and see the envy on the faces of the staff officers. Most very rarely ventured out of the headquarters, where they were trapped behind their desks. They got their biggest kicks from being passengers in one of my vehicles – if, that is, they had a legitimate reason to go into the International Zone and if their colonel would permit them. The majority were stuck in Camp Victory for six months. They lived in the building next to the headquarters. Although many had interesting jobs, playing a part in overseeing Australian operations in the Middle East, they were still desk jobs: none was as good as mine – and they knew it.

Because there were so many headquarters staff, about eighty at any one time, they generated a lot of their own work internally in addition to their actual roles. Jokingly they were referred to as the 'self-licking ice-cream'.

Headquarters staff had rules for when to wear body armour and when to wear helmets and what to do during this siren and that alarm. We just wore body armour and vehicle helmets most of the time. They had rules for when to have your weapon unloaded, when to carry a magazine on your rifle and when to fill the fridge with more water. At the Flats we carried our weapons loaded all the time and filled the fridge when it was getting low.

I was busy. A short trip out on the road as a crew commander was a real luxury. Most of the day I spent in the command post, tracking my vehicles, developing the movement plan for the following day, and receiving requests from the embassy, the Australian headquarters and the Australian military staff working in the International Zone, mostly in the US headquarters.

Some days the movement plan resembled a jigsaw as I tried to piece it all together. There was so much to coordinate: the ambassador needed to be at the UK embassy the same time the general needed to be at the US embassy. The signallers needed to be at the brigade combat team headquarters as part of a monthly classified equipment check and the special operation liaison officer needed to go to LZ Washington, the helicopter landing zone in the International Zone. And one of the ASLAVs needed a 10,000-kilometre service, which involved an engine lift, so it'd be off the road for the day at least. Honestly, this was not what I had trained for back in Australia. I was a cavalry troop leader trained in armoured manoeuvre, but many days I found myself working in a mix of roles, from liaison officer with the embassy and movement and logistics coordinator to operations officer dealing with random problems as they arose.

It was confusing and I buggered it up a few times. Once, the ambassador didn't get to where he needed to be on time, so he called my boss. He yelled at him about what a crap job we were doing, then my boss in turn yelled at me. That was how the chain of command worked. Generally, though, things worked.

The boys spent a lot of time on the road; there were always 'fast ball' tasks that came up throughout the day.

Common sense tells you that the greater your exposure to dangerous activities, like driving around Baghdad, the greater your chances of bad things happening to you. And we were close. I don't know how many times.

Once for sure. Key trouble spots were the checkpoints into the International Zone. The International Zone housed many of the interim government's administrative buildings and also many of the city's famous monuments: the Monument to the Unknown Soldier; the El Haria (Liberty) Monument in Baghdad's Tahrir Square, commemorating the 14 July 1958 revolution; and the Victory Arch, commemorating the Iran–Iraq War, which consisted of a pair of hands holding crossed swords.

To the east and the north, the International Zone was secured by seemingly endless rows of 9-foot cement 'T walls', with all roads leading into the zone heavily controlled by the Coalition and the Iraqi army and police. The checkpoints were named on a somewhat clockwise basis, checkpoints 1 and 2 to the north, checkpoint 11 to the south, and 12 to the west. They also took on colloquial names, such as 'Assassins' Gate' for the checkpoint that led to the entrance of Haifa Street or '14 July checkpoint' for the one leading to the 14 July Bridge.

One day, one of my crew commanders radioed in that he was approaching Checkpoint 12. As a deterrent, this checkpoint had an Abrams tank with its barrel pointing towards approaching vehicles. It didn't work.

Approaching the checkpoint, the Australian patrol identified a suspicious vehicle driving strangely, which they thought might contain a suicide bomber. They accelerated into the checkpoint to prevent the vehicle getting close. As they entered the chicanes, the vehicle detonated among the cars queued in the civilian traffic lane.

I heard the explosion from the Flats, even though it was about 2 kilometres away. The crew commander had radioed through that they were approaching the checkpoint. Then, again on the radio, we heard: 'Fuck, that was close.'

A massive smoke plume billowed up from the carnage.

These attacks were not uncommon. But there were also other hazards we never thought to consider. An American soldier dropped dead at Checkpoint 12 only a week or two after this incident. They had decided to do twelve-hour piquets (guard duty shifts) and he had taken only one litre of water with him. The temperatures were over 40°C during the day, and he was alternating between standing in the sun and sitting on a tank under a makeshift shade. They said his muscles just liquefied and the heat killed him before they could get him anywhere near the hospital.

*

Of course, not every Iraqi was trying to kill us. Mohammad downstairs, the building caretaker, was a lovely bloke. So was Fil, our interpreter and the go-to man for any local services or contractors we needed. The children that waved on the streets were like children anywhere in the world – cute, happy, smiling . . . But my specific dealings with locals were generally unpleasant, and this was not necessarily the fault of the Iraqis. Rather, it was because one of my jobs was to receive compensation claims from locals who had had their vehicles damaged by us.

As noted, we drove hard on the roads and would regularly nudge vehicles out of the way. The trim vanes on the front of the vehicle – designed to extend when the ASLAVs entered the water and keep the vehicles afloat – bore a kaleidoscope of colours from the paint scrapes of the vehicles we had hit.

When we struck a local vehicle on the road, if it was tactically sound to stop, which wasn't often, we handed the driver a form that allowed them to apply for compensation for the damage. It was a crazy system. The principle was sound – to help people repair the vehicles we had damaged – but I'm certain that in a lot of cases things didn't pan out as intended.

The system had been in place since just after the first SEC-DET arrived, and by now all the locals knew about it. So we would regularly get people turning up to try their luck. I would listen to their claim and if it matched an incident that one of our crew commanders had reported, I would give them a form to fill out. The flipside was that if we had been unable to stop and hand out our claim form, and if I was unable to match the damage to a specific incident, we couldn't process a claim. I am sure there were plenty of legitimate claims that didn't get processed.

These exchanges tended to be emotional and many of them went against much of what I had been taught. According to our cultural training, all Iraqi women wore burqas and walked with their eyes down two paces behind their men. We were instructed never to look a woman in the eye. If you wanted to address a woman, you should talk to their male companion and put your question through him. We had been told that if you talked to a woman or looked her in the eye you would offend everyone and the only way for her to regain her honour and her family's honour, and to save your own testicles from being detached by an enraged brother with a sharp knife, was to marry the girl.

Therefore I was alarmed one afternoon when a call came that there was a local woman at the side gate who wanted to discuss a vehicle damage claim with me. When I opened the steel door at the side of the Flats, I saw two women standing near our infantry soldiers, with no male chaperone in sight. Both were agitated; the closer woman had, I think, been tapping her foot while waiting for me. Both were well dressed in a corporate style, wearing trousers and jackets with bright-coloured headscarves that showed their full faces, and they had no male chaperone. This was not what I had been told to expect from Iraqi women, which, again, confirmed my doubts about some of the 'experts' who had briefed us before our deployment.

I grabbed Mohammad on the way out, assuming I would need a local speaker to help me through the discussion. But when I greeted the women, they both returned the greeting in fluent English with a slight American twang. I thanked Mohammad and let him return to his small stall that sold $5 cartons of cigarettes, cases of Coke and locally made leather pistol holsters.

I asked these women into the Flats, as I was never comfortable having long conversations out on the street. I took them only to the first floor, where our dining hall and kitchen were situated and where we could sit. They explained that their vehicle had been hit and badly damaged, and gave the date and location of the incident. I left them with a soldier and went to the command post to check the records. Nothing matched, and I had to tell them that we had no record of the incident and therefore were unable to pay compensation. The conversation went nowhere but round in circles, and the women got progressively more distressed. I finally got them to leave, but they weren't happy.

And they weren't the only ones. Some days saw a procession of people claiming compensation: some with legitimate claims, some with obviously bogus ones, some whose claims had been approved but who were waiting for the bureaucratic cogs to turn and provide them with a few hundred dollars to repair the damaged panels and front suspension from having an ASLAV strike them from the side as they entered a roundabout, and some who just didn't understand the difference between an ASLAV and the US Bradley vehicle that had hit them. Then there were many like these women, with possibly legitimate claims that just could not be substantiated. I was powerless to help them and they hated me for it – probably hated Australia for it.

I learnt quickly not to use local interpreters like Mohammad or Fil, as conversations would go round and round in circles – apparently this was the Iraqi way of doing business. I tended to use soldiers who had done a three-month Arabic course. They were able to pass on some information but did not allow the locals to repeat themselves. It helped keep the meetings short.

But sometimes it created other problems. Once a small, bent elderly woman started to berate the young digger who was interpreting for me. Even if it was happening in another language, it was easy to recognise the sound of an older woman scolding a young man. I asked him what she was saying. He said that he was getting the words wrong and using the masculine term of address. He said she was saying, 'Stop calling me a man!'

One instance did go well . . . sort of. A man who had visited several times to check how his claim was progressing arrived at our side gate. The message was passed on and I checked the file and saw that his claim had been approved and that compensation would be paid. He was to be well compensated, as he claimed that his vehicle was a taxi and without it he had no livelihood and his family was going hungry. (I had asked Fil about such cases. His response was, 'They are all taxis, particularly if it means you get more money.')

I went down to the side gate to tell this slim, leathery old man that his claim had been approved. The welcome news was translated just as one of my patrols was returning. When he realised he was going to be paid, the old man's hand shot out towards me and I reached to shake it. He grabbed hold and pulled me towards him and kissed me on both cheeks. His stubbly face scratched against mine, and over the vehicle noise I could hear the howls of laughter from my vehicle crews as they rolled into the car park under the Flats.

*

The troop was a mix of characters, from highly intelligent young soldiers through to ones whose knuckles dragged. Many had joined the army straight out of school, but others were older, having worked, some for many years, before joining up. Some were talented drivers or gunners; others struggled with the complexities of working in a dangerous city. Individuals didn't miraculously change when they went on operations: the good operators were still good; the shaky guys still struggled.

But their underlying qualities were twofold. One, they were all professionals. Guns were always clean, vehicles were serviced, ammunition was checked, drills were practised. Even if they did lapse, I had a strong troop sergeant who would fix the problem before I knew about it. Two, they were larrikins – classic larrikins – looking for the humorous side to everything. Spending three minutes with a group of them was likely to leave you in hysterics. Their language was generaly foul, their rooms were plastered in porn and their jokes were always irreverent.

'Hey, fucktard, bet you can't take a taser to the balls.'

'Yeah, righto, do you think I'll blow blanks afterwards?'

Their pride in their job and their unit was seemingly endless. For some, this pride stemmed from the belief that they embodied the Anzac tradition and legend. For others, it was the pride you get from being part of a strong team, from working with a group of men that feel like brothers. And for many it was a combination of the two. They had acquired a small bird, a budgie they named 'Courage', after the 2nd Cavalry Regiment mascot, a wedge-tailed eagle, which was back in Darwin.

Before leaving for Baghdad, the boys organised a squadron

t-shirt. On the back was the motto 'Eruptio Cuius Rectum Nil Liberieum', surrounding a small green foetus wearing boxing gloves. Apparently this was dog Latin that translated as 'Up the bum, no babies'. It was quickly banned by our squadron commander, who, unsurprisingly, hadn't approved the design.

In Baghdad the troop developed a game of stencilling the unit logo, a much more tasteful eagle and lance, wherever they could throughout the city – the concrete walls outside the Ba'ath Party headquarters, the back of a US HMMWV (high mobility multipurpose wheeled vehicle), the roof of the Slayer tunnel. Once we had a tour of musicians and comics visit to 'keep up morale'. When they had finished keeping up our morale, the troop was tasked to carry their luggage and equipment from the second floor back down to the vehicles. By the time the tour left, nearly every case and bag had been stencilled with the unit logo.

Discipline was never a real issue in the troop – I was always the sort of commander who would let things like harmless stencilling slide. There had to be a bit of larrikinism. I rarely had to speak to anyone about a disciplinary matter, as I was lucky to have a strong troop sergeant who sorted most issues out before they ever got to me. I got on well with my sergeant; there was a mutual respect between us that bordered on friendship. Generally the more weighty discipline issues were beyond my authority anyway – like when one of my soldiers accidently fired off a 9-mm round into the unload bay as he was about to clean his pistol. Charges for unlawful discharges went straight to the major commanding the combat team.

There was a bit of 'us and them' among my cavalry troop, the military police close personal protection team and the infantry platoon – these were the three main groups within the 110-man combat team. The delineation of command was always an issue. The military police argued that they were closest to the embassy staff we were protecting, so therefore they should command every patrol and situation involving the embassy staff. The infantry claimed they provided the local area security to the embassy, so they should command and make all decisions for the Flats, the embassy and the Carthage Hotel, a local hotel where the embassy staff, including the ambassador, lived. My crew commanders always believed *they* should command all patrols, including when the embassy staff and military police were involved.

I don't recall there ever being any real resolution to this, and at times it caused some heated debate. I don't believe the major commanding the combat team ever weighed into the debate either.

The infantry soldiers, in their role providing local area security, had a long, hard four-month tour in Baghdad. While we spent a lot of our time on the road, seeing the city and beyond, they spent their time rotating between static security positions around the Flats, the embassy and the hotel. This was only occasionally broken by foot patrols around the neighbourhood. Otherwise they sat behind machine guns in windows on the third or fourth floor of the Flats, or at the front gate of the embassy, or at the front security desk of the hotel. They were long, slow days.

The monotony and boredom got the better of at least one young soldier. While on late-night security at the hotel, he chose to relax a bit. His orders were for him to remain at the desk, alert, with his webbing and body armour on, while the embassy staff slept in the hotel rooms above. He was the last line of defence after the Iraqi private security team that ran the checkpoint leading to the hotel, who were generally considered poorly disciplined and untrustworthy. Rather than adhere to his orders, this young soldier was found fast asleep at the desk, with headphones in his ears and his rifle and ammunition under the desk in front of him.

Witnessing how this case was dealt with, I questioned, for the first time, how effective military discipline was, and how ingrained and contrary to good command the military legal system had become. Rightfully, this soldier was landed with a serious charge that saw him returned to Australia to spend fourteen days at the defence correctional facility at Holsworthy – military jail. But after that, rather than being sent back to his unit in disgrace, inexplicably he was sent back to us in Baghdad. This soldier, who had been negligent in his task of providing security for the embassy staff while they slept at night, was returned to continue the job. The legal officers had insisted that not returning him to Iraq could be construed as a second punishment, a form of double jeopardy, because he would miss out on the deployment allowances. For me, it was obvious, even common sense – if you take off your webbing, put your rifle at your feet and your headphones in your ears, then allow yourself to fall asleep while providing security to the embassy staff, clearly you do not have the required training nor frame of mind for the job and you should be returned to Australia for retraining.

Sadly, this was not the only time I questioned legal interventions in military decision-making, nor the only time that I would see soldiers fail to take their responsibility seriously. The extravagant deployment allowances for operational deployments seemed to lead some to see themselves as more like mercenaries than soldiers.

6

TASK TO AL KASIK

AL KASIK IS A SMALL TOWN IN THE NORTH of Iraq, situated about halfway between Mosul and Tel Afar, not too far from the Syrian border. The town, which seems to materialise out of a patch of desert as you approach, is on low ground, but the whole area has the high craggy mountain range of Iraqi Kurdistan as its northern backdrop.

Al Kasik, originally an Iraqi army base, had several monolithic structures, in stark contrast to the flat treeless environment. These buildings were home to an Iraqi army brigade, and through 2004 and 2005 the Australian army had a team working to mentor and train the Iraqi soldiers. While they had some initial successes, later, after their task changed in 2005 and they were withdrawn from Al Kasik, the Iraqi brigade regimental sergeant major (RSM) was kidnapped and publicly executed. This event triggered the informal disbanding of the brigade, for the simple reason that the soldiers were too scared to turn up to work.

While the execution of the RSM was the final straw for the Al Kasik brigade, it had been plagued from the start by seemingly minor issues that then snowballed. For example, the civilian kitchen staff served a variety of poisonous dishes that Iraqi bellies could hold down, but Australian bellies could not. These staff were paid more than the local soldiers who served on the base. So while the kitchen staff ensured massive weight loss in the Australians, they also collected a large pay packet. This caused extreme ill feeling among the Iraqi soldiers towards the kitchen staff.

Perhaps the pay discrepancy was warranted. Before my arrival in Iraq, a large truck bomb had detonated outside the dining facility one lunchtime. Somehow, this explosives-laden truck passed through several checkpoints, drove to the top of a dirt mound next to the facility and detonated its cargo. The blast tore through the corrugated iron building and many of its occupants during the crowded lunch. The number of fatalities and casualties was extreme, and among the victims were many kitchen staff. When I arrived in Al Kasik, many of the Australians were still a bit shaky from the experience.

*

The Phase 3 ASLAV happened to come into service while I was in Iraq. The job of rotating out the old Phase 2 vehicles fell on my shoulders. There were about twelve ASLAVs all up in Iraq: seven in Bagdad and five in Al Kasik. What this meant was that I would have to drive five new Phase 3 vehicles half the length of

Iraq, so they could be swapped at Al Kasik, and then drive the Phase 2 vehicles back. If I had been a bit older and a bit wiser, I probably would have told someone to fuck off. But at the time I saw it as an opportunity for adventure – with the bonus of being able to meet up with a good friend who was a member of the training team.

He had been married less than a year before and I had been best man at his wedding. As was common, he had had to leave his bride soon after they were married: within a couple of weeks he left to attend a three-month language training course in Victoria, then, after a short return home, he was deployed for six months to Iraq. We had seen little of each other since training together at Duntroon, so we were keen for a coffee and a chat and any excuse to smoke the cheap Iraqi cigarettes.

My five-vehicle patrol, about twenty of us all up, left the Flats at first light, making our way through the city to join Highway 1 and head north. Our maps were bad and our communications even worse. I had a satellite phone to communicate with headquarters – if the batteries held out. I had been given a bunch of frequencies on which to contact the Coalition's quick reaction force in the areas we were going through. I was lucky we had a crew commander who had driven the route before, because the directions were poor and I really didn't know what to expect.

We stopped briefly at Balad, near the old armoured-vehicle graveyard, and I asked some US soldiers what frequency they had for the quick reaction force. It was different to the frequencies I had been given, which confirmed my suspicions that if we got in trouble we were going to have a tough time calling for help.

We drove up through Samarra and Tikrit, stopping at small US forward operating bases to get fuel and check on the condition of the road north. Some of these little bases were getting smashed with regular indirect fire, and the routes in and out had seen regular IED strikes.

Highway 1 was mostly one lane in each direction and the traffic flow was constant. Every so often we would pass burnt-out trucks on the side of the road. As we passed one truck, my gunner remarked, 'Look, that bloke's asleep in front of his truck.' I had already noticed the man as we approached, and commented back, 'He's not sleeping, mate . . .' It wasn't clear how or why he had been killed, but from his blood-soaked face, his lifeless body as vehicles sped by within metres of his head, and the dark patch of blood that stained the asphalt around his body, it was clear he had met a violent end. The road – in fact the whole country – was pretty lawless.

As we travelled further north, the population thinned out and the boys wanted to test-fire their guns. I kept my eyes out for a deserted stretch of ground on which to loosen a few rounds off, but it seemed that every crest revealed open desert with a handful of mud huts with satellite dishes on their roofs. I didn't want to take any chances, nor did I think it was fair to terrify these poor villagers by firing a burst near their homes. So we continued on, getting to Al Kasik by late afternoon.

We were exhausted when we arrived, but we did some work

to get the old vehicles ready for the return trip the next day. I met with my friend, drank some coffee, smoked a few cigarettes and stayed up too late.

My friend explained to me that they had been issued with new vehicles just before the attack. These were parked near the dining facility, about to be handed over to the team, when they were torn to pieces by the blast. Instead, the training team was given little Eastern European four-wheel drives that were 'agricultural', to say the least. My friend had decided to personalise his by unbolting the roof and doors.

I always felt uneasy in the big dining facilities. Hundreds, sometimes thousands, of soldiers all jammed in the one place. Easy targets. There were constant stories of suicide bombers targeting these buildings, and rockets would often be fired by insurgents at about lunchtime in the hope of a lucky strike. Hearing about the recent attack at Al Kasik confirmed my fear of eating in such places, and throughout the tour I never unloaded my pistol before going to meals.

I woke the next morning feeling tired and unenthusiastic about the long day ahead. One of the vehicles being replaced was a personnel carrier with the old swivel-mounted .50 calibre machine gun, which I stupidly said that I would crew on the trip home. I tried to do the right thing as the boss and take the worst car, but this was a mistake. If we got into trouble, I would have my hands full just trying to control the heavy gun in its old-style mount, let alone commanding the patrol.

Luckily, the return trip was uneventful – relatively speaking. There was some crazy high-speed driving, and the Iraqis showed me just what poor drivers they were by doing things that nearly had me running them off the road or shooting them in fear they were suicide vehicles. A prime example was when a fuel truck pulled out in front of my lead vehicle. I assessed the situation and thought, 'This could be an ambush – a big truck cutting us off. All they need is a few RPG teams on the side of the road and we're in trouble.' I had the safety off the .50 calibre and was close to letting a few rounds go when I thought, 'Fuel truck . . . armour-piercing incendiary rounds . . . this will not end well.' So I rode it out without firing, and it turned out to be an ordinary truck driver who did not know how close he was to having his vehicle turned into a fireball.

We all got back exhausted and keen not to do that trip again.

*

By now I had been in Iraq for three weeks, and I was becoming more comfortable with my role. I didn't have much opportunity to consider the bigger picture of what we were doing there, nor how the insurgency was affecting everyday Iraqis, nor where Saddam Hussein might be hiding. I didn't have time to consider what the embassy was actually achieving in the country, but I did think that their morning bacon-and-egg barbecue on the front lawn of the embassy in the middle of Ramadan probably wasn't endearing us to many of the Muslims in the neighbourhood.

In just over a month we planned to be back in Al Kasik for the second half of our tour, but as with so many plans made in wartime, this one didn't turn out as intended.

7

THE ATTACK

I WAS THE PATROL COMMANDER FOR THE SECOND task of the day on 25 October 2004; the first had been to pick up the embassy staff from the hotel where they were staying. The weather had started to cool a little, and as we pulled onto the main street the warm orange sunlight hit my face. As we drove out of the Flats, I remember thinking to myself what a beautiful morning it was.

The traffic was flowing steadily at 8 a.m., like in most major cities of the world. My two-vehicle convoy roared down the main street that runs east to west and divides the Karadah Peninsula. The task that morning was very much routine: a drop-off in the International Zone, a pick-up at Camp Victory and back to the Flats. While we regularly travelled with no-one in the back of our vehicles, on this day the front vehicle in the patrol had an extra vehicle crew: three men (crew commander, gunner and driver), one of whom happened to be my troop sergeant. We were also carrying an IT technician from the Signals Corps, which were affectionately referred to as 'geeks'. After I dropped off the geek in the International Zone, I would head to the Australian headquarters at Camp Victory to drop off the extra crew.

It was the sort of routine job done by my three patrols up to twenty or thirty times a day. When I look back on it now, I have trouble believing how naive we were to be running what is best described as an armoured taxi service around Baghdad.

My patrol hit the main two-lane roundabout midway down the peninsula with turrets spinning and horns blaring. Roundabouts created utter chaos in this city. There seemed to be no rules except that the biggest vehicle had right of way. Our vehicles were inevitably the biggest and we had a general rule that we stopped for no-one.

We came out of the roundabout and accelerated hard, down a wide, tree-lined street with cars parked along both sides. As we passed one of them, the bomb inside it was triggered.

Of the explosion I remember nothing. Our vehicle careered into a tree, and uprooted it. I must have been unconscious for only a few seconds and came to with the thought that I had been shot in the head. On the ASLAV Phase 3, the hatches folded back to horizontal, unlike the older vehicles with hatches that locked vertically. This meant you could turn and look behind you, but were without the protection provided when the hatch was sitting up straight behind your head. My first troop sergeant, who had done a tour of Baghdad some four months earlier, had told me he saw no good reason for folding it flat, as it took away the extra protection and you could be shot in the head from behind. But I had chosen to fold it flat. Therefore, when I came to, I instantly assumed that he had been right and that I had been shot in the head from behind. It was a relief to find this wasn't the case, but I still couldn't breathe or see.

I had never been knocked out cold before. I had no understanding that after such a blow to the head you just drop. When I looked through the blood into the bilge below the turret cage of the vehicle, I realised that I had collapsed, and the pain in my legs was from having them twisted underneath me in a tangled mess on the floor of the turret. I quickly clambered up onto the ammunition bin in the centre of the turret and, once seated, tried to think straight about what to do.

Although I was no good to anyone, I started shouting at my gunner to get the radios working. Unbeknown to us, the blast had tripped the circuit-breakers in the vehicle, so that we had no radio, no power, nothing. I later discovered that both my gunner and driver were doing a brilliant job of fending off the crowd of locals who had gathered around our stranded vehicle. I was blinded and not helping anyone by yelling about the radios and that the two vehicles at the Flats should come and support us. My crew wisely ignored me.

My driver and gunner were out on their own, with their troop leader wounded on the streets of Baghdad and a growing crowd. After incidents like this, crowds could turn violent very quickly.

The number of wounded from this blast was never confirmed, but many locals suffered gruesome injuries. While the locals understood that we were not directly responsible for the bomb going off, their thinking was that if we had not been there to be targeted, the incident would not have happened. It was with such thoughts that a large, volatile crowd gathered, many members of which had just seen family members, friends or neighbours killed or hideously wounded.

*

Later, back in Australia when I had recovered, the men described to me what they saw that day. The two local children who would run out to the footpath to wave each time our vehicles passed disintegrated when the bomb detonated. One second they were running, smiling and waving enthusiastically at us as we passed. Then, in a blink of an eye, their little bodies were torn apart and their flesh and body parts showered the roadway.

A man staggered and dropped, one arm severed at the elbow, the skin and muscle from his face hanging from his chin. The red-hot, razor-sharp fragmentation from the bomb had ripped through him and he died there on the footpath.

Seemingly instantaneously, the crowd surged around the bomb site, angry, crying, shouting. A news crew jostled to get footage.

*

I have since seen video from the Australian snipers on the rooftop of the Flats as they tried to raise my callsign on the radio from within a thick wall of dust that surrounded the site. The other vehicle in my patrol had lost all radios when the explosion occurred; its vehicle circuit-breaker had tripped too. The drill was to travel to the nearest Coalition checkpoint and try to fix the problem. Within a couple of minutes they had reset their circuit-breaker and returned to where my vehicle had come to rest.

I don't recall too much of the next minutes. I forced open my eyes only a few times. Each time, I was greeted by the same sight: walls of dust, angry locals, a handful of Australian soldiers attempting to keep the crowd at bay, shouting, chaos.

An Al Jazeera news crew was on the scene within a minute or two of the blast. They were lucky to avoid being shot by one of my corporals. It may have been chance, they may have just been in the area, but the boys' tempers were boiling and when they saw a news crew arrive within moments of the blast, they assumed insider knowledge.

The quick reaction force was sent from the Flats, less than a kilometre away, and arrived with two additional vehicles and the medic. It was only a couple more minutes before a US Bradley patrol also arrived to add to our cordon and help secure the area. The boys helped me from my vehicle and into one of the other ASLAVs. While my head and neck were a mess from fragmentation and burns, my body was alright apart from sprained ankles and raw knees. During the transfer, one of my lance corporals was guiding me, but he had to stop to speak briefly to one of the US soldiers, so he directed me to wait beside the vehicle. Thinking

I knew better and would make my own way into the back of the vehicle, I kept walking, staggering forward, thinking I knew the way even though I could not see. He swore and grabbed me, stopping me from walking straight into the crowd.

Once I was in the back of the vehicle, the medic gave me a shot of morphine and my gunner stuck his head in to check on me. I remember thinking that the buildings to our east had been named in several intelligence reports as possible insurgent hideouts and I told him to watch for snipers from those buildings. Stupid. The dust was so thick that snipers wouldn't have had a chance of seeing anything. I was still trying to be a commander, not realising I had lost the ability to command shit.

They had me to the Coalition Support Hospital (CSH – referred to as the 'cash') within twelve minutes. On the way there I held a blood-soaked dressing to my face and tried to make small talk with the medic. Stupid again. By that time I could barely string words together, from a combination of shock and morphine.

I don't remember arriving at the hospital, but apparently when the medical staff asked how I was doing, I replied, 'Peachy.'

It was lucky the day did not end differently. We were there to protect the embassy staff. My patrol was the second of the day. The first had been tasked with picking up consular officials and taking them to the embassy. Their patrol had passed the IED strike site about five minutes before mine did. Would it have been mission failure if the IED had gone off next to the vehicle with the ambassador in it? Yes, I think so. Was the IED targeting the

Australian embassy staff? Maybe, but in that case they had done a shit job. The ambassador travelled in an armoured BMW back then – he was an easy target.

8

BLACK HAWK TO BALAD

IN THE CSH IN BAGHDAD, THEY SLICED OPEN my neck to get to the internal bleeding that had given me a grapefruit-sized lump in my neck by the time I got to hospital. They also cleaned out the big chunks of fragmentation and asphalt that had penetrated through my forehead and into my sinus cavity.

I don't remember much of the forty-eight hours in the CSH. I remember some high-ranking US officers visiting and giving me two unit coins, something US soldiers prize – little tokens with unit insignias on them. After a sleep, I woke to find only one of them remaining.

I caught sight of myself in the mirror a few times and was horrified. My head had swelled so much that I looked like a bear. My eyes had closed over from the swelling and I had to force them open with my fingers and clean out the accumulation of gunk before I could see anything.

I remember lying there crying at some stage: I don't know when or why. Maybe it was shock. Maybe my painkillers were wearing off. I can't remember.

One of the infantry corporals dropped by to give me a mobile phone. Although I recalled the dialling codes for Australia, I couldn't remember anyone's phone number except that of my best friend in Sydney, whom I had spoken to only a few days earlier.

I finally got through to him, and when he spoke I realised I had no idea what I should tell him, and I felt sick in my gut. All I remember getting out was, 'Some cunt tried to blow me up.' We spoke, but not for long. I don't remember what we said to each other. Bloody painkillers.

The doctors decided that I needed to be evacuated out of Iraq. I was flown by helicopter up to Balad, the first stop before flying on to Germany and the massive US medical facility that received all casualties from the Middle East.

The night-time flight out of Baghdad in a Black Hawk was truly one of the more unsettling experiences of my life. I had spent the last two months in body armour and with a pistol strapped to my leg, always ready to defend myself or others. Now they fastened me naked to a stretcher, covered only in a blanket. I had no pistol and I was drugged up to the eyeballs, so if something happened I wouldn't be able to do a thing. I remember taking off from the CSH helipad thinking, 'This is fucked . . . please don't go down.'

At Balad, I was seen by a doctor at the triage tent just off the side of the runway. I was deemed able to travel and they had me on a C-17 to Landstuhl military hospital in Germany that night. The plane was full of casualties from all over Iraq. We lay in rows of rattling stretchers, with medics constantly moving up and down the aisles checking our stats. They kept pumping us full of painkillers.

That was how I left Iraq the first time.

*

Crystal had planned to travel to Spain with a friend in late October. The day before she was to fly out, she was walking in Hyde Park, London, when someone from the army called to inform her that several Australian soldiers had been wounded in Iraq. They indicated that families of the injured would be informed within the next hour. An hour passed, and no-one called, so Crystal naturally assumed I was OK. She was further reassured that it wasn't me after checking the Australian Defence website, which had released a media statement saying that the families of the injured had been notified. So she had assumed that I would call her soon. She was anxious to find out more, as she knew everyone in the troop, and was worried about the families back home.

This was the first of several mistakes that occurred because I was the first Australian casualty in Iraq whose wounds were serious enough to warrant evacuation through Germany. My case tested out many of the processes Defence had put in place for such an event, and in several cases proved them to be inadequate. But the first problem was, in part, my own doing.

At the time, the military had a policy that next of kin would only be informed with permission from the injured soldier. It was a policy that I don't think had been well thought through. In Baghdad, as they rushed me into the operating room, I was asked if my next of kin could be informed. At the time, I felt I was thinking straight and could speak, so I figured it would be best if I told Crystal myself. And then they stuck something in my leg and the anaesthetic kicked in.

So there I was, out cold, in surgery, followed by hours in recovery doped up to the eyeballs on drugs, and I had denied the military permission to inform Crystal or my family of my condition.

Crystal assumed I was fine after not hearing back from the army; my mother was not so easily reassured. She had attended an information session before my deployment and had my commanding officer's phone number. I had specifically not put her down to be notified in an event such as this, as I thought Crystal and my sister would be better at dealing with things and keeping Mum informed. But her mother's intuition went into overdrive when she didn't get the answers she was after from my CO. She called brigadiers and generals (some of whom still ask after her – 'Hello Major. How's your mother?'). She made such a fuss, as mothers do, that I think it was assumed she was my next of kin. Eventually someone made the decision that my family should be informed, so they told Mum I had been injured.

But they forgot to tell Crystal. She only found out when my sister called her later that day. On answering the phone, Crystal immediately said how relieved she was that the injured Australian soldier was not me. My sister stopped her and said, 'No, it *was* him.'

We were lucky that I had two close friends working at the Australian headquarters in Camp Victory. Both knew Crystal well and soon passed on what they could about my condition and what was going to happen. For want of a better idea, she was told to go to Spain as planned and they would update her from there.

Crystal spent a cold night in Spain, then flew to Germany the next morning. She was met by the Australian consul general and driven to Landstuhl.

She later explained to me that she had felt numb through this whole time. When she spoke to my sister and finally understood that I had been injured, she returned to the apartment in London where she had been staying with friends. They were all out and she sat there alone, unable to process what had occurred, knowing only that she needed to get to Germany to see me. She decided that she wasn't going to take anything about my condition as fact until she saw me. She had the feeling that once we were together, everything would be alright.

*

I was in the hall when Crystal arrived. I saw her walking towards me. Crystal's a small girl, and as she approached down the long, white hospital corridor she looked tiny.

She seemed to slow down as she approached, a wary look on her face, and I realised that she was not sure if it was me. My face was a mess, and my head was still so swollen that I was unrecognisable. I remember trying to smile and say something stupid, then holding her for a long time.

*

Crystal had walked the long hallways of the US hospital in Landstuhl before she got to me. Even as a nurse, she was dismayed by the sheer numbers of wounded she saw as she came through the hospital. It was multi-storey and seemed to be kilometres across, with every room filled with casualties from Iraq.

She was able to stay locally, within the grounds of the hospital, in a house that had been established to accommodate military families while their loved ones were being treated. Crystal's feelings were mixed about the charity housing. While she was grateful to be able to stay there, she was also overwhelmed by how well equipped the facility was to support injured soldiers' families. It was an obvious indication of how often the house was used.

*

I spent another five days in Landstuhl, where I had another operation. Twice a day I would be dosed up with painkillers and have my face scrubbed with peroxide to get dead skin from the burns off, to prevent scarring.

I was in a room with two others. They were both young marines who had been injured at the same time as each other. In fact, there were about a dozen in the hospital all from the same incident – in which one marine had been killed.

They had been in a small forward operating base near Samarra, playing a game of football in the compound during some downtime. Insurgents had fired a mortar that landed in the middle of the game, injuring most of the players. Lance Corporal Gomez, a hyperactive, skinny little bloke, had been the section medic and had run several hundred metres back to their barracks to get the med kit. It was only as he was returning to his injured mates that he realised his foot was flapping around as he ran. He had copped a fair-sized mortar fragment that had broken his ankle. His mate in the room, Private McLaughlin, had got a piece in his thigh – he was not taking it as well as Gomez, who had requisitioned a wheelchair so that he could make his way down the corridor and out the exit to smoke cigarettes. They both talked constantly about when their Purple Hearts would be presented. Although they were joking, it was inevitable that they would receive the medal for being 'injured in combat', and it was common for US soldiers to be awarded these medals while still in hospital.

My father, an ever-travelling professor, had been at a conference in Austria. On hearing of my injuries, he got on a train and met me at the hospital within a couple of days of my arrival. Both Crystal and Dad spent a lot of time with me. They were amazing.

Crystal, as a theatre nurse, could interpret the high-speed delivery of my prognosis and planned treatment from the overworked US doctors. I had second-degree burns to face and neck, multiple fragmentation wounds to face and neck, a haematoma to the right side of my neck that had required emergency surgery in Baghdad to ensure blood supply to my brain, and puncture wounds to my sinuses, caused by fragmentation. One of these fragments had also fractured the bone between the sinus and the cerebral cavity, so the doctors were concerned about infections in my brain.

During the explanation of the planned treatment, we were told that they were looking to operate again. They explained that as the bone between my sinus cavity and my brain was fractured, they intended to remove this bone and 're-seat' my brain.

Neither Crystal nor my father was happy with this.

The American staff treated me like any other casualty – and rightfully so. But they thought the best place for me to undergo further treatment would be mainland USA. Crystal spoke up, saying that anything they planned do in the US could be done back in Australia – therefore I should be sent home.

Crystal called friends in Australia to get names of hospitals and neurosurgeons back in Australia to further her case for getting me home, and Dad also stepped in. As I was the guinea pig for the casualty evacuation process, and this scenario – an Australian casualty in Germany needing ongoing surgery and treatment that could not be done in Germany – had not been anticipated, the Defence hierarchy was slow to act. Dad spoke to both military and embassy staff. He accused one high-ranking diplomat of being 'the man without a plan' and, using his own credit card, bought two business-class tickets back to Australia, one for Crystal and one for me. He informed the embassy staff and Defence about what he had done and told them we would be on the plane.

During this time Crystal smoked cigarettes from Gomez, and she and Dad walked a fair distance to get off the 'dry' base so they could get a six-pack of beer. Both were anxious and shaky, and in need of their own 'medication'.

Thankfully, Dad's course of action was politely agreed to by all, and Defence picked up the €30,000 bill for the tickets, much to his relief.

*

I travelled back home with Crystal and an Australian nurse, who had been sent to oversee my care. She carried an ample supply of sedatives and painkillers, which would allow me to sleep for much of the flight to Sydney.

A black SUV took us to the Frankfurt airport, where we were shuffled into a private waiting room. At Sydney airport, we cleared customs on the plane, then were escorted out to a waiting car. With all this special treatment, Crystal said she was starting to feel like Posh and Becks.

I had a final operation at Liverpool Hospital in Sydney, where thankfully they chose not to 're-seat' my brain. I had some very competent surgeons, with experience in similar injuries, usually from car accidents where drivers hit their head and face on the steering wheel.

My recovery was surprisingly fast. The stiffness in my body, particularly in my neck, both from having been thrown around in the blast and from the surgery, eased after a couple of weeks.

The swelling in my face subsided, but I was left with what the surgeons described as trauma tattooing – blue-grey marks across my forehead and eyebrows from the fine bits of dust and muck that were embedded in my skin in the blast.

I only got wobbly once – when the surgeon in Sydney pulled out the packing in my sinuses without warning or anaesthetic, then gave me a mirror to gaze into my own sinus cavities.

I stopped smoking – nothing like a couple of weeks on morphine to kick a nicotine habit. One afternoon in hospital, I caught myself thinking, 'Didn't I used to smoke?'

One event from my recovery stays with me in particular, and it was the start of my understanding that, after a bomb blast, the human body is always going to have some quirks. At the time it was absolutely humiliating, but I have come to see the funny side of it. It occurred after I was released from hospital on convalescent leave. Crystal and I went to stay with my sister at her unit in Queenscliff, Sydney, which looked down over Manly Beach. It was the perfect place to recover and start to feel like a normal person again.

I had travelled back from Germany in a cream tracksuit two sizes too big and ill-fitting slip-on shoes – donated clothes from a US charity. I must have looked appalling walking through Singapore airport with my swollen, battered head and dragging my feet to keep my shoes on, all the while in an oversized tracksuit.

In Sydney, I was issued with an army tracksuit and runners, and Mum and my sisters bought me a couple of t-shirts. So all up

I had two bad tracksuits, a pair of running shorts, a set of army runners, a couple of pairs of socks and a pair of slippers. I did not have any underwear.

On one of my regular visits to my doctor, I had asked if I could resume some kind of fitness routine. He said yes, just nothing that had the potential to injure my face or neck. So the next morning Crystal and I decided that we would go for a run along the Esplanade at Manly. It was a beautiful November day, a little bit chilly first thing, but the morning warmed quickly, and soon the Esplanade was full of people out enjoying the sunshine.

I didn't want to push myself, as I was still pretty sore, so we did a brisk walk down the stairs from Queenscliff to the footpath that follows the beach. Here we broke into a light jog and I felt the relief that follows escape from being cramped inside for weeks on end. Crystal trotted alongside, and we quickly made it down to South Steyne.

When we reached the end of the beach, I started to feel a mild need to go to the toilet. We turned and headed back to Queenscliff. We passed the South Steyne toilets and I contemplated popping in for a quick toilet stop. But at the time it was merely a mild pressure and I had no cause for alarm. So we continued to run north, back up the beach.

It wasn't long before things became urgent. In hindsight, I should have turned and run back to the South Steyne Beach Clubhouse and gone to the toilet there. At the very least I could have run into the surf. But no, I left Crystal, muttering that I needed to go to the toilet, and picked up my pace to a sprint in the hope that I would make it to the facilities at the Manly Beach clubhouse. The pressure rapidly became more intense.

On this beautiful, sunny morning, with the beach and the Esplanade full of people, I must have been quite a sight – in ill-fitting clothes, a raw scarred face, sweating profusely and running through the crowds, desperately trying to make it to the clubhouse. To my right, they were doing work on the beach volleyball area on the sand and a large section was fenced off. Even if I wanted to run into the water to relieve myself, I couldn't get to the beach anyway.

Finally, as I stumbled and lurched past the holiday-makers and people out enjoying the sun, the American ration-pack dinner, tinned fruit and one slice of pizza I had been holding for three weeks (the last time I had properly been to the toilet) forced their appearance. At this point, the lack of underwear became critical. About 100 metres from the Manly Beach clubhouse toilets, the poo slid down my leg, as I desperately lumbered my way along the Esplanade. The most unfortunate result was that the sticky poo slid down to my ankle and as I ran through the crowd I kicked it and it whizzed through the air just in front of a female jogger coming the other way. She gave me a quizzical look mixed with astonishment and a touch of disgust: the look of a person who has just grasped that the person running past them in the opposite direction has shat himself and kicked a piece of poo in her direction.

With the bottom half of my body soiled, I ran into the toilets, where I remained for a good twenty minutes, while Crystal waited outside, unaware of what had transpired. Afterwards, with spots of brown on my white t-shirt, bad American army shorts and new white runners, I sheepishly walked back to my sister's house. Crystal pieced together what had happened as I sulked (there is no other word for it) alongside her.

I laugh about it now, even using the story as an icebreaker in uncomfortable situations, but at the time I felt supremely humiliated, and it took me quite a while to come to terms with what had happened.

*

For the two months after my final operation, I lived in a strange limbo, trying to recover, while also apprehensive about what the blokes were going through in Iraq. I was constantly questioning the severity of my injuries – irrationally I was thinking: *surely my injuries aren't that bad? I should ask to go back to finish the tour.*

I received snippets of news: the troop had been in two ambushes during their time at Al Kasik. No Australians were injured, but during the second ambush they had unleashed with everything, all the firepower in the troop, and the US later reported that they killed eleven insurgents.

Only when they had all returned to Australia did I feel I could rest properly.

PART II:
IRAQ
2006

9

GOING BACK

CRYSTAL SMASHED PLATES IN THE BACKYARD when I told her I was going back.

We'd moved from Darwin to Brisbane; it was supposed to be a respite posting with a quiet reserve unit in the suburbs. But circumstances overtook us, and all eyes were on the Brisbane regiment to man the next security detachment in Baghdad.

Crystal went through the classic stages of grief when I told her I had volunteered to return to Baghdad. First, she was quiet for days, then anger saw all our crockery methodically smashed, piece by piece in the backyard. After she finished trying to talk me out of it, then was miserable for a few days, she finally accepted that I was going. She had every right to grieve: she was losing me for another six months, and, as she knew better than most, there was a chance she could lose me forever.

I was being pigheaded, as always. Somehow my injuries and all the pain and surgery hadn't dampened my enthusiasm for returning to Iraq. I was still itching for adventure and wanted to do the job for real. I even felt a little robbed that my first deployment had been cut short.

Except for breaking the plates, Crystal handled the crappy situation I put her in with nothing but class. She focused on planning and looking forward to our wedding, and making the most of our time together. She knew that soon pre-deployment training would consume all my time.

*

In the lead-up to deployment, our instructors used images of my IED strike and lectured us on 'not setting routines the enemy can target', unaware that the surly newly promoted captain with the scarred face sitting in the front row didn't appreciate their advice.

Foolishly, I took Crystal to an information seminar run by welfare officers and padres. She was so tough through all of it. It was only when someone said we needed to keep our contact information up-to-date so that he didn't deliver bad news to the wrong house that she started to cry.

I did get some leniency; I was excused from attending the three-week reconnaissance into Iraq that would be the first stage of our handover with the outgoing combat team. My commanding officer decided that, as I had already been to Baghdad, my spot would be better taken by someone else. The news came as an enormous relief to Crystal and me, as the reconnaissance had coincided with our planned wedding date.

We married in early November 2005 and had a short honeymoon before I commenced training for deployment in March.

*

For most of the junior soldiers, this was their first overseas deployment. But I found myself in a strange situation for a junior officer: I had some credibility with many of the soldiers already.

Generally, lieutenants and captains have to work hard to gain credibility, particularly with the non-commissioned officers – the corporals, sergeants and warrant officers – many of whom have served for considerably more time than junior officers. But many of the NCOs saw me as a hardened veteran.

I felt this credibility was completely undeserved. As far as I was concerned, I had got myself blown up – it was nothing to revere.

Rumours even began to circulate: that I was a great tactician; that I only slept a couple of hours a night and lived on coffee. The most ludicrous I heard was that I had thrown someone from the balcony in a nightclub fight. I got to work one Monday morning and some soldiers wouldn't make eye contact with me as I passed them.

Many of my friends just joked that I was 'going back for a re-test'.

Meanwhile, my mother, completely unintentionally, added to her notoriety with many high-ranking officers. During her long and emotional discussions with several generals following the IED strike, she had managed to get General Leahy, the Chief of the

Army, to promise I would not be sent back to Iraq. So when my name was confirmed on the formal deployment order, I sheepishly approached my commanding officer to inform him of the promise that had been made to Mum.

The military cogs turned: my commanding officer called the brigade commander, who then called the land commander, who then spoke to General Leahy. Luckily, he saw the situation for what it was – he had told an emotional mother what she needed to hear during a very traumatic time. Through my brigade commander, he confirmed that I was volunteering to go, then passed on the message that I should be allowed to re-deploy. He also indicated that if my mother wanted to discuss the matter, he would happily contact her.

To Mum's credit, after a call from me to explain what was happening, she didn't take up the offer.

*

I boarded the plane to go back to Iraq eighteen months after I had first deployed. By then, I had recovered completely from my injuries, except for a few scars and some little quirks – I had permanent pins-and-needles down the right side of my jaw, I was very susceptible to sinus infection, and, as it turned out, the incontinence I first experienced on Manly Beach was an enduring physical ailment I would have to learn to live with.

During those eighteen months, I had spent considerable time training those going to Iraq. I was the one who told them what it was really like there. I would curb their enthusiasm by showing them photos of my injuries, videos of how they were going to operate, and telling them how, yes, people might try to kill them. There was always a noticeable change in the soldiers after my presentations: a shift from the childlike enthusiasm of looking forward to a big adventure to a sobering realisation of the environment they were about to enter. A friend of mine described it as 'watching the arse drop out of their showbag'.

As executive officer of the next security detachment, I no longer interacted as much with soldiers; I didn't have a troop, as on my first tour. Instead, I spent my time planning, training and preparing for all 110 of us to deploy. Again, the detachment was made up of infantry, cavalry and military police, with support from a range of other corps – intelligence, ordnance, signals, and electrical and mechanical engineers. We also had a couple of cooks.

I spent more time with the officers, as I would need to give daily direction to the troop leader and platoon commanders. They were a mixed bunch. The infantry lieutenants came from the 3rd Battalion, our parachute regiment – a unit with strong *esprit de corps*, forged by scaring the piss out of themselves by jumping out of planes. The two lieutenants were like chalk and cheese: one was a loudmouth from a military family; the other a pensive man, a trained physiotherapist. There was also a quiet cavalry troop leader and an opinionated military police captain. We all got along pretty well, but the driving force behind the combat team was the Boss.

He was older than most company commanders, just ticking over into his forties. He had discharged as a captain and made his way very successfully in the private sector before returning to the army – he just missed the job.

The Boss's age gave him a wisdom that most majors seemed to lack. To say he was a father figure to us is not right – he wasn't that old – but he was a true mentor. He had a sharp mind and was as comfortable talking with generals as he was with private soldiers. He was one of those genuinely amicable characters – unless you crossed him. Then he would focus all his intellect and energy on calling you out and discrediting you and your opinion for all to see. He took his role and responsibilities very personally.

As much as he could, he developed relationships with the soldiers. He really wanted to know about their wives or girlfriends, and to get the boys' opinions on matters: how they felt about this and that. It was what made him so well liked, but may also have led to the problems when we returned – once the dust settled and life moved on. His self-questioning, his guilt over what he may or may not have done – it broke him.

But as we readied to deploy, the Boss was the embodiment of strength. If you put all 110 of us in a room and asked who would suffer from post-traumatic stress on their return, he'd have been the last one you'd pick. Events would show that it's not about mental weakness, it's not about physical strength and it's not about intelligence. It's about individuals and circumstances, and how different people react differently.

10

BACK IN THE MIDDLE EAST

ONCE AGAIN THERE WERE MONTHS OF TRAINING, AND exercises – this time conducted around Brisbane – intended to replicate the job in Baghdad and expose us to every conceivable contingency: from changing ASLAV tyres in a hostile area to suicide bombers detonating at the front gate. We never trained for a soldier accidentally shooting himself – that was not a conceivable occurrence.

For our farewell we flew to Sydney: crappy sandwiches and instant coffee, a speech by a general, and then it was time to go.

I don't know why I was so keen to return. I felt that I had unfinished business, even though I couldn't say exactly what that business was. I did know I was the right man for the job.

It didn't seem long before I was back in Kuwait, the desert stretching all around.

Our staging area was Ali Al Saleem Air Base – hot and dusty, with row upon row of tents. The tents ringed the dining hall, as well as fast-food outlets that competed with convenience stores, tailors, barbers and little shops selling trashy knick-knacks. The whole base seemed to have been dumped in the middle of nowhere – it was surrounded by a 10-foot barbed wire fence, beyond which was moonscape desert as far as you could see.

Dust blew through the place constantly. Down one end of the base, at the end of a long road that shimmered in the heat, was the airfield. Large transport planes thundered in and out, all through the night and day. The base moved up to 3000 people per day in and out of Iraq – and then later Afghanistan.

The dining hall on the base had the worst (some considered them the best) of the culinary delights offered by Mr Kellogg, Mr Brown and Mr Root – KBR, the bunch tied to the notorious company Halliburton. They fed thousands each meal, and the food tasted like it. The short-order line was for all things fried and grilled: burgers and chips mainly. The long-order line was stews and steaks and the occasional odd offering: tray upon tray of lobster tails or pigs' trotters. One night there were crab claws – the Boss had one for dinner. The company sergeant major joked that as water was so far away, it must have been sand crab. The claws were enormous – how or where had they found them? There was no way I was touching one.

The Australian logistics unit had a fenced-off section of the base that they called home. There were a couple of office buildings where the staff managed the endless flights of people and equipment, a lecture room for final lessons and updates for those going forward to a war zone, and recreation areas, including a big television room where people transiting could relax. So much of people's time in Kuwait was spent waiting. There was a good aspect to this: with all the people coming and going, I was constantly running into people I knew.

On one of our first evenings there, I managed to get on a phone for a few minutes' conversation with Crystal. A small, demountable building was allocated as the 'welfare' room. It was partitioned with plywood walls to make three phone booths and a handful of internet terminals. If you listened, you would hear conversations ranging from teary, affectionate dialogue between family members to arguments over bills, or gossip about what was happening in the 'married patch' in Puckapunyal, Townsville or Darwin.

I had a good talk with Crystal. She sounded happy enough. She'd started a new job assisting with cardiac surgery. She was learning a lot in this new field, and was busy – long hours and shift work – and she had regularly volunteered to be on-call through the night. It all helped take her mind off the separation. Again, I had left her with just Girlie, the dog, who was now in her mid-teens and really showing her age.

*

Outside the base, the barrenness of the desert had its own beauty. Seeing the Bedouin camel-herders, I thought maybe I could enjoy life here, for a while at least. These Bedouin lived a nomadic existence. Their homes were demountable, corrugated-iron structures

Urban range, Kuwait.

on the back of medium-sized trucks. Except for the fact that they were living within the live-fire danger traces of the ranges (where fired rounds could land), it was very peaceful. Most had their families with them. They carried a collection of bathtubs, which they scattered around to water their beasts – usually about ten to twenty camels.

During one of the first days in Kuwait, the company sergeant major hoped to conduct a shoot with our two snipers, but the Bedouin had moved their trailer homes into the danger area, preventing the snipers from firing. Briefly I thought that perhaps we could work on the policy of 'big desert, small bullets', and take our chances that in such a vast expanse the snipers would be unlikely to hit a camel or its herder. But in the end my conscience won out. And I later discovered that if you killed a Bedouin's camel, you paid him not only for the camel, but also for the next three generations of camels – which equates to quite a sizeable sum.

Later we went out to the 'urban range' in a procession of air-conditioned buses. This was a patch of sand divided by berms into 20-metre-wide corridors. In the corridors were mock houses. The idea was that life-sized targets were placed in the buildings, and groups ranging from two to five moved through from one end to another, firing at the targets. As safety officer, I would move along the narrow walkways atop the structure and shout directions as required. The biggest problem was again the Bedouin, who let their animals graze at the end of the range. Most of the rifles shot out to more than 3 kilometres. The area was also littered with unexploded ordnance: I saw an 81-mm mortar sticking out of the sand. Whenever you use a range in Australia, you are briefed about the dangers of old ordnance: 'Don't touch them, kick them, don't even cast a shadow over these things, as they might go off.'

The Boss and I went out to move the Bedouin and their camels out of the danger area. We kept to the existing vehicle tracks that crisscrossed the dunes, hoping this way we would be less likely to trigger any old munitions. Our plan was to drive from truck to truck (there were about ten, spaced about 500 metres from each other) and ask them politely to move off so that we didn't shoot them.

Our first two attempts to move the herders out of the danger area met with lethargic, uninterested responses. I don't think the Bedouin spoke English, and we had no interpreters. The Boss decided to try a bit of Arabic himself next time, with the aid of the *Arabic at Your Command* book we'd been issued. But to our surprise the third Bedouin truck was not owned by an Arabic-looking man, but by a dark African who spoke perfect English. It didn't matter: he was equally immovable.

At that point, we gave up and I practised saying, 'I have diarrhoea' in Arabic instead. While it gave us a laugh, it also had a practical purpose: I had learnt I needed to be prepared for my overactive digestive system.

*

The evening saw a visit from the new Minister for Defence, Dr Brendan Nelson, who had commenced in the role only a few weeks earlier. He met with us and exclaimed how fit we all looked. We were taken aback – it sounded a bit fruity. But then, considering we were in the company of the logistics unit staff who supported operations in the Middle East, full of truckies and storemen, well, we probably did look fit, so we decided to take the compliment in the spirit intended.

Nelson spoke very enthusiastically to the gathered crowd, clearly passionate about his work, but tending to say a bit too much. He spoke of how happy reserve soldiers would be about new pay incentives. But we were in the Middle East; there were no reserve soldiers here to be impressed by the increase. While I thought Nelson was a genuine person, I found his lack of awareness of his audience and the environment disconcerting. It seemed he was being let down by his military advisors. Later, as our time in Iraq progressed and circumstances unfolded, I think this poor support from his key military advisors got him into trouble, especially when he talked to the media.

We also met the brigadier commanding all Australians in the Middle East. He came across as an unassuming character who cracked a few jokes and seemed very relaxed.

The Australian army was finally getting over a period termed, by another brigadier, 'the great peace'. Since Australia's involvement in the Vietnam War, the army had deployed only a handful of times until the early 1990s. And then we had not sent troops away in any organisation larger than a battalion group – around 600 people – up until the deployment to East Timor in 1999. The result was a cohort of senior and non-commissioned officers who had never seen real conflict, let alone been tested by it.

But now we were seeing the end of this peacetime legacy, with officers making it to one-star general rank who had, for example, commanded soldiers in Somalia in 1993 and battalions in East Timor, and were therefore less risk-averse and reactive than many of their superiors.

Luckily, both brigadiers who commanded during our six months in Iraq fitted this new mould. They were strong characters, who responded to bad news by embracing the problem and seeking to solve it. In this, they differed from many high-ranking officers, whose response was to fire a volley of questions at the commander on the ground, only adding to the friction.

*

A Hercules flew us into Baghdad International. After briefings at Camp Victory, we were herded onto a Chinook for the flight into the International Zone. We watched the city lights whirl by out the back of the open tail of the giant helicopter, where the loadmaster sat with his machine gun.

I was amazed by how much things had changed in eighteen months. During early 2005, the security detachment had suffered a further two significant IED strikes. The first was a suicide attack on a convoy on Route Irish that had badly damaged a vehicle and left several soldiers wounded. Some had the grisly affliction of bone fragments and flesh from the suicide bomber embedded in them.

Later, a second bomb detonated at the front of the Flats, laying waste to the Hesco baskets (the large dirt-filled mesh baskets used as protective barriers) that surrounded the Flats. Soldiers had been sent flying, with several requiring treatment and one being sent home with spinal injuries.

The Australians had then packed up and moved into the International Zone. I was thankful not to have been part of that shitfight. An entire embassy and its staff, all the soldiers and all the equipment that had been brought into Baghdad for SECDET had to be moved. They shifted 110 soldiers, rations, vehicle spare parts, beds, desks, radio equipment, satellite dishes, memorabilia, tools, paperwork, the ruggedised photocopier . . . everything.

SECDET's new home was an old Republican Guard barrack. The area, renamed 'the Cove' after Anzac Cove, was a series of single-storey brick buildings ringed with a brick and T-wall fence. One long building, running almost the length of the area, was used as accommodation and a single larger building near the entrance was the headquarters and command post.

The toilet facilities in the headquarters were closed off, because the sewer was broken. One was turned into the armoury and the other had a desk and safe and was used to store sensitive information and communications equipment. The young female signals corporal who worked in this area, named 'the vault', was not happy about having her workspace positioned over a toilet in which Iraqi army soldiers had once defecated.

There was a workshop and garage for our vehicles. We had ASLAVs, up-armoured four-wheel drives, unarmoured or 'soft' SUVs, an enormous Ford F-350 up-armoured ute, and an old Nissan Pajero given to us by a private security force. The Pajero was a cheap up-armoured vehicle that the contractors had rolled while practising counter-ambush drills around the Crossed Swords. It had dented panels and the doors didn't close properly, but it was a favourite with the team's two snipers, as it was fairly inconspicuous when they drove around the International Zone. By contrast, most of the Coalition cars were shiny black humvees or big, white suburban SUVs with black tinted windows.

The Ba'ath Party headquarters, a monolith of a building, was located about 100 metres from the Cove. It had a massive hole through the middle where a rocket had struck but not detonated. Standing in the basement, you could look up and see daylight. During our time in Baghdad, the hole was patched, even though what appeared to be structural girders had been badly damaged. The area where the nose of the rocket must have lodged was turned into a small water feature and surrounded by a food court and trinket shops.

During our handover, I went to the US embassy to meet a few of the Australian 'embeds'. Embeds were Australian staff officers performing roles within the Coalition headquarters. I heard it said many times that the embeds were Australia's 'main effort' in Iraq.

While we had 110 soldiers in SECDET, another 600 or so made up the Al Muthanna Task Group further south, the Australian Army Training Team Iraq, and the Australian headquarters at Camp Victory, to name a few of the larger groups. Out of all these, the individual staff officers holding key appointments within the multinational headquarters gained the most impact flying the flag for Australia, as they got the most exposure to our Coalition partners.

The US embassy was a beautiful old building, one of the oldest in the city. It had an outside pool that attracted all kinds. Walking past, I saw girls in bikinis sunbaking on deckchairs. Since this embassy was the target of most of the rockets that were fired into the International Zone, I had to wonder if they fully appreciated where they were and the danger they were in. The scene was quite surreal.

The new Australian embassy was positioned not far from the American one. I remembered walking through the shell of this building just after consular staff had acquired it in 2004. A lot of work had been done since then. There was a lawn to one side and the soldiers were accommodated out back, in demountables positioned under a concrete rocket screen.

On the other side of the embassy was the Coalition Support Hospital, where I had spent a blurry forty-eight hours in 2004, undergoing surgery and getting pumped full of painkillers. The staff rotated regularly, but I met with the commanding officer of the hospital and explained that I had been a patient eighteen months earlier. I thanked him for what his fellow countrymen had done to help me. He seemed very appreciative.

I had been planning to visit the hospital ever since I'd been told I was going back to Iraq. But when I finally got there, I was surprised how little I recognised. Nothing brought back memories. I even went into the emergency triage room where I had first been taken. Nothing. In hindsight, I should have expected this: while I was there, my face had been bloodied and swollen, and I had only been able to see when I prised open my eyes with my fingers.

*

SECDET, the combat team, was separated into two groups, with most of us at the Cove, and the second platoon and the military police at the new Australian embassy about 2 kilometres to the east. We were all within the International Zone, which gave us, at one level, an element of security. There was little chance of car bombs in the International Zone, but, as the Boss put it, it was 'like having all your eggs in the one basket'. The majority of the rockets fired around the city were aimed at the International Zone. Chances were the insurgents would hit something important – an Iraqi government building, an embassy or a military headquarters building.

Although the media would report later that we lived and worked from a 'barracks', our little world in the Cove and the embassy was nothing like a barracks. We manned checkpoints there, we had overwatch positions with machine guns, we kept weapons on us at all times, and we lived under constant threat of rocket attack and random fire. While in some respects it was safer than living on the Karadah Peninsula, it was still a dangerous place and if you had to call it anything it was a 'forward operating base'. But we quickly made it our home and got to know our new neighbourhood – the stretch on the north-western side of the Tigris that was the International Zone.

*

One of our first planned tasks was a trip out to the Flats. A 'nursery run', they called it, to familiarise the new blokes with the environment and to get some dirt in their teeth before we had any real tasks to complete.

I wanted to check on a couple of things. First, there was Mohammad, the caretaker of the building. When the Australians occupied the Flats, Mohammad lived in the style of a rich man. It was said that he owned the Flats, which, if true, would have made him very rich. In any case, his sale of cigarettes, Coke, pistol holsters – just about anything in fact – gave him a comfortable income.

But when the Flats were abandoned, so was Mohammad. It was common for people who worked for Coalition forces to be killed. I thought it likely he had been killed in reprisal for assisting us. So when I got to the old gates at the ground floor of the Flats, I was happily surprised to find him still there. He was obviously struggling financially: the little empire he had built for himself had crumbled. He recognised me when I approached and greeted me warmly, shaking my hand vigorously and saying that he had not known what happened to me after that 'big boom'.

He asked me who else was with me in Baghdad, and I mentioned a few men from earlier deployments whom he might know. He was very excited and asked me to pass on his regards. Clearly he thought there was a chance we might move back to the Flats. He kept asking me for a job in the embassy. I had to tell him I would look into it, but I knew I would not. If the embassy staff had not taken him when they left, they would not take him now.

Second, I was curious what had become of the building that so many Australians had called home. I took a look around. It was very eerie. The dusty rooms were empty and unlit. What had once been home was now a dilapidated warren of dark hallways. There was almost no sign that we had been here. In fact, I had to look very hard to find anything. Up on the third floor, through a couple of corridors, I came to the room that used to be the 'Cav Room', a common room with a TV for the cavalry soldiers, a place to relax and jaw off. I had given my nightly briefings there.

It would have been just a nondescript room, like tens of others in the building, except for the red wall. It had been painted red when the company sergeant major was looking for ways to entertain the soldiers, particularly the infantry men, who spent most of their time in static defence positions around the Flats and the embassy. One of his ideas was to have a competition for the best-decorated room. A couple of coats of red paint on the main wall in the room, a white frame and the addition of a gaudy tiered fish tank/waterfall, and the prize was theirs.

The red wall was the only sign I found that the Australians had been there.

*

I had been sure that I would be fine to drive past the site of the incident, but when it came down to it I wasn't really. When we left the Flats, the patrol headed back towards the International Zone using the exact route that we had taken the day of the incident eighteen months earlier: east down the main road, then through the roundabout and north towards the 14 July Bridge and the International Zone checkpoint. I was in the commander's position of an ASLAV, as I had been on the morning of 25 October 2004.

Suddenly, as we approached the depression in the cracked road that had been the seat of the blast, I had an overwhelming thought – or rather a question: *what if it happens all over again?* What if, at that moment, another bomber was sitting in a window looking down on the road. What if, at that moment, he was poised to press the button that detonated another carful of explosives? The road was full of parked cars, and it was near impossible to tell a vehicle bomb from any of the other cars parked by the road.

It was an irrational fear that welled in me, and I had to fight to stay standing in the turret. I knew that if I ducked down, I may as well have stayed at home, because at that moment I would have been no good to the patrol. Instead, I watched in a mild state of terror as we drove past the cracked footpath, the poor brickwork that had been erected to patch the damage done to the nearby houses, and the uneven space in the row of trees on the median strip where my vehicle had come to rest after hitting and uprooting the large tree.

As I watched, I had instantaneous recall of events. I imagine the same thing happens when a person's life flashes before their eyes. But it was the aftermath of the incident I relived, that minute or so after we came to a stop. Not being able to breathe. Not being able to see. The pain in my legs. Forcing open my eyes and looking into the dusty floor of the turret.

My sergeant leaning into the turret and asking me how I was doing.

The dusty street and the crowds . . .

And with those flashes, my head cleared and I was back on the road, with the knowledge that maybe I was not as tough as I thought, and a sense of relief that nothing had happened in those few seconds, because if it had, I would not have been in the game.

The last stretch of the route back into the International Zone passed without incident. I got back to the compound a little shaky, but feeling that I had faced a few demons that day – demons I hadn't been expecting. Maybe I was even a little stronger from the experience.

11

A JOURNEY AND A BOXING MATCH

IN 2006 WE HAD THE FEELING THAT WE WERE part of history in the making. The insurgency in Iraq was at its height; it dominated the Western media. The city was constantly abuzz with helicopters overhead. Car bombs thumped the city on a daily basis. Rockets regularly fizzed through the skies and cracked into buildings in the International Zone.

Every day, a procession of black SUVs and a large black bus trundled in from Camp Cropper, bringing Saddam Hussein to the trial being held, ironically, in the back of the old Ba'ath Party headquarters, just over our back fence.

The checkpoints to enter the International Zone still had lines of cars waiting to get cleared, and also much pedestrian traffic, creating long lines in the mornings.

In 2004 the checkpoints had been manned mainly by US soldiers. They were regularly cleaned up by suicide bombers, who had little trouble driving to a checkpoint and waiting in a queue. When a soldier approached their window to check ID, they would detonate the explosive load in the boot or on the back seat, taking with them the soldier, to meet God or Allah or whomever. I always felt extremely sorry for the nervous soldiers manning the checkpoints as we drove through; their fate was determined by the time they drew on the roster. Any vehicle that pulled up at the checkpoint could very well blow them to pieces, or maim them terribly in a fireball, peppering them with bits of vehicle and artillery casing.

In 2006 the checkpoints were still under constant attack by car bombs and snipers. But the tactics had changed somewhat, with several 'tiers' in place to process the cars. The outer tier was usually manned by Iraqi private security, who would do a cursory check of the vehicle and wave it through to the next tier, which was most likely manned by Iraqi army or police. After a more detailed check, the vehicle would either be waved through, past the Coalition soldier behind a machine gun pointed down the line of waiting cars, or directed to an adjacent area for a more detailed search.

At the checkpoints there were constant 'escalation of force' incidents, in which a person was shot if it looked as though they were a suicide bomber. On several occasions, checkpoints were the sites of 'assisted suicides'. Once, an Iraqi man approached the 14 July checkpoint in a suit with a briefcase, which he opened, drawing a replica pistol and pointing it at the US soldiers on guard. I thought that in a gun culture like Iraq's, a replica pistol would probably be harder to come by than a real one. He was shot dead.

*

Tasks outside the International Zone were called 'Red Zone' operations. They were usually either reconnaissance for an upcoming task or transportation of embassy staff to a ministry or embassy. Both involved significant planning by the command team, both officers and NCOs. We'd sit around the large conference-room table and methodically work through the threats and insurgent trends in the area we were about to enter, even to the point of breaking down schematics of the venues.

We would then assess what vehicles and men we had available while still maintaining enough for protection tasks around the International Zone. Following that, we came up with several plans – covering patrol configuration, timings, routes – in as much detail as necessary. The Boss (or I, in his absence) would weigh up the advantages and disadvantages of each plan and select the most appropriate one. We would 'war-game' the plan through each phase, considering what the enemy could do and how we would react. I would then develop written orders detailing all the coordination and timings to make sure no-one was confused.

Many tasks were extremely complex and synchronised down to five-minute intervals, with several vehicle patrols and sniper teams inserting early and feeding back real-time images of a venue, and advance teams securing the venue before the diplomatic party arrived. Others were very simple, particularly if the venue was just outside the International Zone, which many were.

I laughed to myself about how much things had changed from 2004 to 2006. Back in 2004, we'd had two or three patrols on the road all day, every day. Rather than doing detailed planning, we'd worked off a matrix indicating which patrol needed to be where and when. It was very loose, and therefore dangerous. Back then, we naively ignored the intelligence sergeant's warnings, and heard about all the strikes on Coalition patrols but assumed it would never happen to us. The opposite was true in 2006. We planned in detail, drawing greatly on the intelligence sergeant's assessments and statistics. I was the only one in the combat team who really understood how differently we operated compared to eighteen months earlier. I was quietly reassured that the level of planning guaranteed that we operated in the safest way possible in such a dangerous city.

So much was going on these days that I didn't get much sleep, but I loved the job. Life was busy, but also full of unforgettable situations. While I had told everyone back home, particularly Mum and Crystal, that I would be spending the entire six months behind a desk in the command post, sometimes I couldn't help myself and had to get back out on the road. People believe what they want to believe, and I think Mum and Crystal were happy believing my lie.

One was a task to Kirkush, an old Iraqi army barracks and staging area used especially during the Iran–Iraq war, where two Australian warrant officers were helping to train an Iraqi army battalion. We had been tasked to deliver equipment to that remote little pocket in the desert, which had a range where we planned to fire off some of the vehicles' older ammunition.

I took the commander's position in the turret of one of the sergeant's vehicles, at the rear of the six-vehicle convoy. My job was to maintain the link between the convoy and the headquarters in Baghdad and coordinate any Coalition forces if we got into a fight, or had a breakdown or accident. But with all the radio jammers used by the militaries around the city, it didn't take long for our radios to drop out. I held on tight to my satellite phone. While there were three radios in the vehicle, I had a feeling the phone was now the only reliable means of communication.

Kirkush was about 20 kilometres from the Iranian border, and it took about three hours to get there. The route was lush and green as we followed the Tigris north out of Baghdad, but then we headed east and green turned to brown. The people changed too. The waves became stares, and the stares became glares. Many turned their backs, and others made indecipherable but obviously unfriendly gestures. There was nowhere more dangerous in Iraq than Baghdad. But these people, even the children, hated us.

The journey led us through Baqubah, a Sunni insurgent stronghold that had seen fierce fighting in 2004, as violent as in Fallujah and Ramadi but not on the same scale. It felt like most of the city's 500,000 inhabitants were on the main street as we drove through – and they had hate in their eyes.

After hours on the hot road, Kirkush appeared out of the scorched desert: just another Iraq barracks built on a seemingly nondescript patch of dirt. The familiar series of big, rectangular, monolithic buildings was the same as I had seen at Al Kasik on my first trip. The ground was flat and brittle. The weapons range was a patch of desert facing out towards a mountain range on the horizon, which marked the Iranian border.

We met the two gruff old warrant officers; they had been there for months already, with little contact with Australia. Strangely, they didn't seem all that happy to see us. I think they felt like kings of their little domain and our arrival challenged that; it was a little primal. We headed out to the range, as we didn't have much time if we were to make it back to Baghdad before dusk. One of the warrant officers started to get funny about us not having a range safety trace, a drawing on a map to indicate the arcs and direction we could fire. This was a safety requirement, showing that you had cleared the area into which you were intending to shoot.

The range had seen decades of use, not to mention the real battle that had been fought there with the Iranians, and there was no way I was sending anyone out to risk being blown up by the scores of unexploded bombs. It was a patch of desert. We could see pretty much all of the area we were firing into and we could see if anyone was moving in the danger zone. I politely explained to the warrant officer that our having a trace would achieve nothing and we were firing anyway. There was some hesitation – 'But sir, siirrr, I don't think I can let you fire.' At which point we ignored him and got on with it.

We fired all the old 25-mm ammunition, about 200 rounds per vehicle, then reloaded for the drive home. We fired some old 66-mm shoulder-fired rockets that had been rattling around in the vehicles for too long, and some of the 40-mm grenades. The snipers ranged the sights on the new rifles that they'd just got in from Australia. We were finished in just under two hours. It felt a little crazy firing off large amounts of ammo in the direction of the Iranian border.

The run home was long and painful and dangerous. I couldn't help noticing that the attitudes of the civilian drivers on the roads had changed a lot in eighteen months. Where once they had jostled around the vehicles, trying to cut us off, or driven right up behind us, at least until we pointed the 25-mm barrel at them or waved our pistols, now they swerved off the road when they saw us coming. No-one came within 100 metres of the ASLAVs.

The introduction of the US forces' informal policy of 'get too close to my vehicle and I'll shoot you' was obviously working. It must have made for a very bad day for some.

*

Being an officer was always challenging; it required a fine balance between relating to and interacting with the soldiers, and not getting too close. You had to maintain your credibility as a commander who made life-and-death decisions, while being empathetic to your soldiers' wants and needs – and also know when to tell them to shut up and get on with the job.

While sometimes it could be a bit lonely, especially when you had to make unpopular decisions, I always relished being the one who called the shots – I hated being a follower.

SECDET's two platoons of infantry soldiers were from specialist platoons – reconnaissance, assault pioneers, signals and direct first-support weapons (also known as heavy weapons). This meant that they were all senior soldiers, having served three or four years each.

It was great to have more experienced blokes with a range of skills. The assault pioneers were constantly building things; the recon soldiers were very methodical and deliberate and provided very accurate reporting, and many could be paired with snipers. The infantry soldiers would regularly escort Australian civilians around the International Zone – a job that required tact and a level head, not just because of the dynamic and dangerous environment, but also because the civilians could be prickly. The downside was that these experienced guys presented a challenge to the chain of command. Some were jaded and surly, and others would question orders. While it was sometimes good to be challenged by smart soldiers, when they were questioning just for the sake of questioning they became hard to work with. Many felt that with three years' experience they knew better than their commanders.

While many were excellent, some proved to be a challenge. They were caught imitating American soldiers by cocking their rifles three times to clear them at the unloading bays rather than going through the correct drill of looking in the breach to confirm no rounds were caught in the chamber. They would position empty Coke cans under the concrete footpad leading to the lookout positions so they could hear when someone was coming to check on them. They would listen to music and miss radio checks. They would take off their helmets to pose for photos in areas where they were in range of sniper fire.

Mostly, they were informally disciplined by the platoon staff – given an extra shift or the next crap job that needed to be done. But one night I lost my temper with two soldiers who hadn't answered a radio check for half an hour. They had been positioned in the overwatch position looking down on the Cove from the corner of the Ba'ath Party headquarters building. A rocket had landed on the other side of the International Zone and I was keen to know where, as we had some Australian civilians working in that part of the city. I knew these soldiers had been sitting up there listening to music on a pocket radio. Many of the soldiers carried these, but they were not allowed to be used on duty. I had to send someone up to get them to answer their radio. Once they finally answered, I ordered them to report to me at the end of their shift.

They both swaggered into my CP, already giving me some ridiculous excuse as to why they had not answered their radio. It was the first time I had yelled in years. Officers generally shouldn't yell, only when a point really needs to be made. They left with their heads hanging and probably thinking I was an arsehole: I had threatened to charge them and see that they were sent home if they did anything like it again. I would like to think that it had some effect on the attitudes of the soldiers; at the very least, many of them kept out of my way for the next few days.

There was an interesting dynamic within the team as a whole. The military police were all senior soldiers, but the cavalry troop had more junior soldiers and a few who had come across from the reserve army to serve full-time. They brought an interesting mix of skills from their civilian jobs – there was an electrician, a barista and a bricklayer. Among the three females in the combat team were two military policewomen who would deal with local women at the embassy. Then there was the supporting personnel: five signallers, including the third female, who maintained our computer and radio links; a medic; mechanics; armourers; storemen; and a couple of cooks.

The officers and senior non-commissioned officers worked hard early on to make sure there was no poisonous rivalry between groups. We trained together; everyone learnt how to change ASLAV wheels and how to work the radios; all the teams gave presentations on their capabilities. We also really pushed the sergeants to work together to set an example for the junior soldiers Previous rotations had problems, which, I felt, stemmed from the soldiers seeing the sergeants not getting on – before they knew it, people were spitting in each other's hats.

And overseeing all this was the Boss. One time he showed his class was during an impromptu boxing match in the Cove. It began with yelling in the compound, and a crowd of people moving out of the new 'Cav Room'. Only a few days earlier they had voted to turn off the 24-hour porn channel, as they were getting a little strange.

I didn't think much of the noise at first; there was always something going on in the compound, with the blokes having a laugh or playing a prank. The group was shouting and moving towards the makeshift boxing ring, just a covered area with a few gym mats and a punching bag or two suspended from the girders that held up the roof.

The Boss turned up in the crowd not long after I did. The cavalry guys had been worked into something like a frenzy, spurred on by one of the sergeants, a hard-as-nails non-commissioned officer who had challenged two soldiers having an argument over who had eaten the last piece of pizza to 'sort this out in the ring'. With the encouragement of the cavalry troop, enthusiastically joined by many of the infantry platoon, the pair were corralled in the boxing ring.

I expected the Boss to be extremely hesitant about the boys having their own boxing match, as the army had all but banned boxing, considering it too dangerous. But he stood back and let the crowd pad the two blokes up. It became obvious that the crowd was far more enthusiastic about the fight than the two participants were. The round started, still with the Boss watching, his calm, quiet demeanour giving nothing away. I was waiting for him to step in any second and break up the fight and chastise the sergeant for provoking the incident. To tell the truth, if the Boss hadn't been there, I would have stopped the fight. I knew that Defence did not look favourably on people getting injured during organised boxing matches, let alone impromptu ones.

But the Boss had made his own quiet assessment of the situation and allowed the boys to let off some steam. A couple of minutes of wild, clumsy haymakers and the fight was over, due to exhaustion rather than any clear victory. It was only then that the Boss stepped out in front of the crowd. I think many of the soldiers were surprised to realise that he had been there all along.

'Who's next?' he demanded. There was instant quiet among the crowd, particularly from those who had been the most vocal during the fighting. 'I thought so,' he shouted. 'It's usually the ones who start these things that don't have the guts to get in the ring themselves.'

With these words, the crowd dispersed, many of the men walking off sheepishly.

I later asked the Boss for his thoughts on the fight and he replied, 'In the first ten seconds I realised no-one was going to get hurt.'

*

Later, I was to say that six-month deployments were about right. Two months to settle in, three months to do some good work and make significant changes, and a month to plan your handover and get out.

About a month and a half into the tour, I felt things had started to hum. The dust had settled. The boys knew their jobs. I kind of knew mine. We all understood our environment sufficiently to do our job as safely as possible. Our world had stopped spinning.

And for the first time we had some quiet days. There was a

day here and there when the embassy staff didn't have meetings that we needed to make happen, and when high-ranking visitors or random incidents didn't absorb all our time.

It was on one of these rare quiet days that all hell broke loose. A single gunshot changed our world, and reverberated all the way back to Australia, altering many people's lives forever.

12

DEATH BY MISADVENTURE

JOURNAL ENTRY, 0409 HOURS, 22 APRIL 2006: *Somehow, in a room with two of his mates, in the demountable accommodation in the embassy, Private Jacob Kovco was shot. The bullet entered one side of his head and exited the other, leaving a much larger hole coming out than it did going in. He died there on the floor of his room with two shocked mates beside him. Another soldier revived him not long after. He was moved a few hundred metres to the hospital, where his mind could just keep him alive and nothing else. After his platoon of comrades, friends and brothers had stood by his bed and said their goodbyes, the machines were turned off and Jacob Kovco died again, in a room full of paratroopers tall and strong – all suddenly crippled.*

The call came through on the radio from the embassy: 'Friendly priority one casualty. Gunshot wound.'

I asked them to say it again. I don't know why: I had understood the message.

I recognised the platoon sergeant's voice on the radio: 'Yes, friendly, pri one casualty, gunshot wound to the head.'

A couple of other people were in the command post, and they all froze when the call came in. I don't know about them, but the back of my neck and scalp burned hot, as has only happened to me a handful of times in my life – times when I realise something terrible is occurring.

The Boss was in the conference room, talking to the two infantry lieutenants. I paused at the door, and they all looked up.

'Friendly Priority One. From the embassy platoon.'

The Boss left quickly to organise a car to the embassy, while the lieutenant in charge of the platoon there followed me back to the command post.

Radio updates were coming in again. 'Evacuating casualty to the CSH, conducting CPR.'

The young lieutenant looked at me and asked, 'Who is it?'

It is against all protocol to send the names of casualties over the radio, but at that moment the rule seemed unimportant. I grabbed the handset: 'Send name, send name of casualty.' I could hear the sergeant on the other end key the handset for a second before answering – 'Kovco.'

*

The first few days after the shooting had an air of unreality about them. Events that seemed impossible, but which we knew were true, cascaded and left us feeling all the more numb.

First, Jake died. He accidentally shot himself in the head while two other men were in the room. Back home, the media went into overdrive when Brendan Nelson made one statement, then appeared to contradict himself. One day Australia was told Jake had been cleaning his pistol, then a few days later it was confirmed that, rather, he had died while 'handling' his pistol. A 'senior military source' added to the confusion with further speculation on how the incident had transpired. Throughout this time, there was background chatter from those who believed Kovco had purposely shot himself. Finally Nelson called for a stop to the speculation, clearly as upset with his own advisors as he was with the media. His call had the opposite effect and seemed to fuel further conspiracy theories and claims of cover-ups.

Second, there was talk of a letter Jake had left for his wife – one of those 'just in case' letters. It was found in the pages of his journal. The plan had been to copy the journal and send it to his wife; the original would be required for the investigation that we knew would be coming. But the Boss felt that he should read through the journal to make sure there was nothing inappropriate before he sent it back. What he found was an entry dated exactly one month before Jake died. It was a premonition of Jake's death. He called it a bad dream, but we know now that he saw into the future . . . and he saw his own death.

He told of seeing himself putting a gun to his head and pulling the trigger; he described the bullet entering his skull and the numbness. But he stated emphatically that this was a bad dream and he did not want to harm himself. He then went on in the manner not of a suicidal or depressed man, but of a happy man, yearning for his wife and children, and talked of the future with them.

In the time after his death, only four of us knew of this journal entry.

Then came the third big event. I was in the command post at the Cove when the phone from headquarters rang. It was for the Boss. He came to the phone, listened quietly for a few seconds, and then let out a 'Fuck', just as he had when I reported Jake's head injury from a gunshot wound.

He hung up and walked out front. I followed.

'They've taken the wrong body back,' he said. Private Kovco had remained in Kuwait in the morgue, while the body of a Bosnian contractor was flown back to Australia in his place.

I would never say that the Boss's demeanour faltered, but there were times when this series of seemingly unbelievable occurrences, the burden of command in such situations and a lack of sleep from answering the phone throughout the night left him raw and tense.

Jake, a good-natured bloke with a mischievous sense of humour, helped us even though he was dead: we all knew he would have seen the funny side of this appalling mistake.

Jake had been a last-minute addition to the combat team. A reserve for the deployment, he had been called up at late notice when one of the other soldiers dislocated his shoulder surfing during pre-deployment leave. Jake had been 'lucky' to get the deployment.

I felt so sorry for Jake's wife, Shelley. His parents were looking for answers; unfortunately, the truth was right there in front of them. There was no cover-up, no conspiracy. Jake died accidentally, and somebody fucked up with the bodies at the airport. But his family's response was entirely understandable. They had been fed a mixture of fact and misinformation. They had been given information before it had been thoroughly checked. Given this and the mix-up of the repatriation of Jake's body, it was entirely understandable that they distrusted the information they were given. But this inevitably led them to make up their own theories about what had occurred.

It didn't help that these theories were fuelled by widespread media speculation.

I felt drained. I missed Crystal. There wasn't the opportunity to call her anywhere near as much as I should. I wished I could hold her as she played her ukulele, clumsily strumming away and singing some barely recognisable song. She would tell me stories and make me laugh, as only she could.

*

Through this time, there was so much discussion and consternation about the investigations that were occurring and going to occur. Whenever I spoke to anyone at the Australian headquarters, I was told a new group of investigators was coming out. I lost track of them all. First, there was an initial assessment by some idiot major, then the military police conducted an investigation, then there was a plan to fly in civilian police. Not to mention the planned board of inquiry.

It had been weeks, but besides the investigator and the soldiers retrieving their essential equipment, no-one entered the room after 21 April. We were later to be accused of hampering investigations by allowing Jake's roommates to retrieve their equipment on the day of the death. But this only showed how little some people understood about working in Baghdad. The alternative was to leave these soldiers without their weapons and body armour, and be negligent in not allowing them to protect themselves.

The room was like a dark cloud hanging over the soldiers at the embassy. They had to walk past the taped-off room many times a day, knowing that it was in the state it had been left in on the afternoon of the shooting: personal equipment everywhere, blood soaked into the carpet, the bullet hole in the ceiling. It made us sick just thinking about it.

I offered to clean it. The Boss had been too close to Jake and had enough to deal with. Eventually the go-ahead came through.

I went to the embassy, where I was met by Jake's platoon commander. He had been smoking a lot since the incident, but seemed OK. The Boss had told me not to let him help as it would be too rough on him emotionally, but he had insisted that he needed to be part of it. I gave in. The Boss would have to trust my judgment on this one. Maybe helping to clean the room would help cleanse him of any (unfounded) guilt he felt. Maybe he thought he could have done something to prevent the incident.

Entering the room, I found nothing I hadn't expected. We worked for about an hour with soapy water and sponges. The room would never be suitable for accommodation. There was the hole in the ceiling for one thing, and the carpet would have to be replaced. But the job was done.

I always felt that Jake dying as he did, by his own hand, but seemingly without reason, played on the boys' nerves. I always felt that there would have been less impact on the group if four, even more, soldiers had died by an insurgent bomb or rocket blast. At least they would have had someone to point a finger at. The deaths would have fitted, been legitimate casualties. Jake's death didn't fit.

No-one knew exactly how Jake shot himself, the actual mechanics of how he achieved it. The bullet had entered behind his ear and exited through the top of his head. It could not be suicide, not at that angle, and not with two other blokes in the room. Not when they had just been singing and arsing around. I am resigned to the fact that I will never understand exactly how Jake did it.

*

As the days wore on, things gradually calmed down. The military investigators and civilian police had all the evidence they came for, and had interviewed enough people.

But then, on 18 May, we were told that a disk containing the draft report into the events and the systemic failure that led to Jake's body being lost had been left in a computer in the Qantas Club lounge at Melbourne. For a long time I accepted this as a 'lapse of judgment' or 'terrible mistake', but the more I considered it, the more I came to see it as pure negligence. Defence has many rules pertaining to the handling of classified information. Sure, some of these rules are ambiguous, some are obsolete, some are even a little weird, but to put a disk with a highly sensitive report in a publicly accessible computer and then to leave it there is plainly negligent.

The loss of the report coincided with another visit by the Minister of Defence, Dr Brendan Nelson. In the mess at the Cove, the brigadier introduced me to him: 'This is Captain Callender. It's his second tour in Baghdad and he was injured the first time here.' The minister asked me what had happened, but then did not listen to the response – one of his staffers was rabbiting something in his ear. I was sure he didn't mean anything by it – he was a busy man and the staffers were constantly in his ear about who knows what – but I confess it irked me a little.

We sat down to lunch on one of the long benches in the mess hall and the minister asked me how the men were going. I had a think and replied that they were 'going OK'.

Considering that a fellow soldier had accidentally shot himself with his own pistol, that we were in the midst of a media melee, with conspiracy theories and accusations calling into question the character of everyone in the combat team, that the wrong body had been sent back to Australia, and that now the investigating brigadier had left the draft report in the Qantas Club for Derryn Hinch to get hold of, 'going OK' was probably a bit weak and unlikely to have provided Nelson with much insight.

Why didn't I give a better response? Truthfully, I don't know. Maybe things would have played out differently if I'd said, 'The boys are pissed off; I am pissed off. Where is the top-cover from the defence hierarchy? Why doesn't Air Chief Marshal Houston stand up for us and keep the media at bay? Why doesn't he give the Kovcos the truth and stop letting them believe that there was some kind of conspiracy? Why isn't he being a leader?'

But I didn't – I told him the boys were 'going OK'.

We organised for the minister to speak to the soldiers, who would then have the opportunity to ask questions. Following lunch, a warrant officer pointed out a group of soldiers huddled together in conversation. They were looking anxious and guilty, but I didn't think much of it – maybe they were surly about being a rent-a-crowd for the minister, I said. The warrant officer, who was more on the ball, replied, 'Nah, those blokes are up to something.'

Nelson spoke for a few minutes on the usual themes: 'You are all doing a good job under tough circumstances', 'Glad you are here looking after the security of the embassy staff', 'Keep up the good work'.

Then, when he asked if there were any questions, a few nervous looks were exchanged and in a shaky voice one of the lance corporals opened with, 'Yes, sir, I think Private —— has a few questions for you.'

These soldiers were after blood. Emotive questions were asked, such as 'What will happen to the brigadier who lost the report?' and 'Will disciplinary action be taken against her?' Dr Nelson struggled to give honest-sounding answers and the men started to grow red-faced and fire questions at the minister as he floundered on.

Then came a classic moment of a sergeant understanding when the boys needed to be put back in their box. He politely excused himself to the minister, then said directly to the soldiers that everyone makes mistakes, that he himself made them every day, and that they shouldn't dwell on the mistake made by the brigadier.

This particular sergeant was much respected by the soldiers, as a mentor and leader, but also a disciplinarian. They all took his point that it was time for them to shut their mouths, because they were achieving nothing. It was inspiring to watch.

I walked Nelson out of the mess.

Years later, I was privileged to have a private conversation with Brendan Nelson, and we exchanged our views of the event. It was only then I truly saw the situation from his perspective. It seemed that the upper echelons of Defence, and the lower, were both having the same discussions – should the senior officer who left the disk in the Qantas Club be disciplined?

I learnt that Dr Nelson's hesitation in answering the soldiers' questions was due to the fact that he was yet to receive a satisfactory answer from the Chief of the Defence Force. He felt, as we did, that disciplinary action should be taken, or, at the very least, be seen to be taken.

In November 2007 the brigadier was promoted to major general. Were political agendas more important to the top brass than fundamental military values and discipline? That is what the soldiers thought.

*

At the start of the tour, the signals corps IT blokes, the 'geeks', had shown me how to use Skype. They set up a wireless network around the Cove so everyone could call home when they had some spare time. Crystal and I would talk every few days.

She would regularly send me video messages. I would go to bed at night watching the little 30-second video clips she had emailed me that day. She would tell me little stories about what she had done that day, or play me something she was learning on the guitar, or just let me know she was on her way out to dinner with friends and that she loved me and missed me.

The military had a policy that if you deployed for six months or more, they would try to rotate you out for ten days' leave. They would either fly you back to Australia or pay for a flight to Rome. Some men were keen to get home for a break, while others wanted a European adventure. Crystal had chosen Rome, so a lot of our conversation revolved around the holiday plans she was making.

She later confided to me that one afternoon she had received a phone call. She answered the phone and was stunned when a male voice asked 'Mrs Callender?' in an official-sounding voice. She instantly assumed she was about to be told that I had been injured, or worse. But the man on the phone turned out to be a travel agent calling to confirm details of our upcoming trip. When she hung up, she was almost sick.

That was how she lived for six months – in a constant state of fear and anticipation. Some couples are different: some are happy to be apart, and some spouses are just glad to have the large deployment allowances that lob fortnightly into their bank account. Crystal and I were never like that. We loved each other's company and it hurt every time we said goodbye.

*

The Boss had been working extremely long hours and I often wondered how he kept it all together. He'd had so much pressure on him from headquarters, and from Australia. Like all of us, he read the online media and he knew what was being said: it was a conspiracy, someone had killed Jake because he discovered a government plot. How had we had allowed it to occur? What were we hiding? What had really happened? He took it all very personally. And there was the guilt, unjustified though it was: I know he felt guilty for Jake's death.

But the tragedy of the matter was there was only one bloke responsible for Jake's death, and that was Jake himself. All the rules were in place that should have stopped him from returning to his room with a loaded pistol. But for some reason he had chosen to ignore them or forgotten the numerous checks designed to ensure that fatigued soldiers didn't walk back to their accommodation with a pistol ready to fire.

The board of inquiry was planned for May and by now the counsel assisting the board had arrived and settled in. There were five of them, all military lawyers, from a range of backgrounds. Together they reviewed our standard operating procedures, spending most of their time tapping away on their laptops in the room out the back of headquarters where we had a bank of computers. After about a week, they were done and we planned their drive back to Camp Victory.

The boys decided to play a practical joke – as soldiers do, jokes and pranks being a way of life. They drove them by ASLAV from the International Zone to Camp Victory. Once they had turned off Route Irish, the practical joke began. The lawyers were inside the base and they were safe, but in the back of a vehicle they had no way of knowing this. As far as they knew, they were still on Route Irish. So the boys started yelling and, out of view of the lawyers, hitting the side of the vehicle with a ball-peen hammer so that it sounded like bullets hitting the side of the vehicle.

The team of lawyers arrived at the Australian headquarters all shaken up. No-one told them it had been a joke. At some stage, the lawyers must have told the operations staff at the headquarters that the patrol had been shot at. The staff would have looked into it, only to find that it was a prank. One of the tasks of the counsel assisting the board of inquiry was to determine if there was any kind of risk-taking subculture within the combat team. After such a practical joke, understandably enough, they believed such a subculture did exist. Their imaginations ran wild.

*

The Boss went on some well-earned leave in June and I commanded SECDET for over three weeks while he was gone. At first I felt like a snotty young first-year captain and expected I was going to struggle. The Boss had faith in me, the headquarters in Camp Victory would keep an eye out, and I had trained to do his job before we left Australia – but there were moments that brought home the burden of responsibility, and the lack of margin for error.

We conducted a Red Zone operation to reconnoitre the German embassy. When we reached the place a local contact had described to us, we discovered that the German embassy had moved a couple of years earlier. This was embarrassing, to say the least, and it was also downright dangerous. There we were: out in the Red Zone with incorrect information. To be fair, this was the reason we did reconnaissance. Far better to get there a week before the meeting to find out the location was wrong than to arrive blind on the day with the ambassador in the back.

I enjoyed running the combat team. It was a rare privilege for a junior captain to be in charge of so many operations. I would have to wait another five years before I was promoted to major and given a squadron of my own.

*

I also decided to buy a goat. The grass was getting long and I thought the blokes could do with a distraction. We organised it through one of the local contractors. It was a cute little thing.

When it first arrived, it took off as soon as we untied it and ran to the back of the Cove to hide among the vehicles. I'd gotten permission from the Boss to get her, but hadn't told many people that she was arriving. Many of the soldiers were stunned to see a goat skipping around among the parked ASLAVs, and there were mixed feelings about the new acquisition.

The goat (photo courtesy of Jim Culloden).

'What the fuck have we got a goat for?'

'That fuckin' goat shits everywhere.'

I'm sure she got a few surreptitious kicks, but as her place in the Cove was endorsed by the Boss and overseen by me, these were always kept out of sight. More often than not, I would walk out of the headquarters and find a group of soldiers giving her a scratch, or watching her jump from the lower narrow ledges of one T-wall to another.

She took a liking to me and slept outside my door, much to the disgust of the intelligence sergeant I shared the room with.

'Fuckin' goat just shat at the door again, sir.'

It turned out that goats are no good at keeping grass short. Who knew? I had in mind that she would keep it nicely trimmed, like on a bowling green. But it seems goats yank grass out by the roots as they eat. So instead she left bald patches in the long grass outside the headquarters building and down behind the accommodation rooms.

There are rules about not keeping animals when you're deployed. It's all about not spreading disease and mange, and apparently having an animal regularly shit outside your door is bad. So we were breaking the rules, but it was a calculated decision. The signallers built her a little enclosure near the front gate, but when any rank visited we tied her up near the back fence. Sometimes there were questions about where the bleating was coming from.

Even though feelings towards the goat were mixed, no-one could deny that she had proved an effective distraction from everything else that was going on.

*

The board of inquiry commenced its hearings a day or so after the Boss returned from leave. He had to travel to Camp Victory to front the board via teleconference at 3 a.m. It was being run on

Australian time – there was no acknowledgment that we were on the other side of the world, trying to run operations.

The men's prank had pissed off a lot of people at headquarters. The Boss had been grilled on his way through.

Of the board of inquiry I know very little. I was so focused on running the day-to-day activities of SECDET that I didn't have much time to think about what was happening. The Boss and the infantry lieutenant would go in and front the board. Then some of the soldiers would be called up, then the military police captain, then a few more soldiers, then the Boss again. I was more focused on transport arrangements for getting them into Camp Victory and back.

*

The goat's tail was getting matted up with poo. It was my responsibility – I couldn't ask anyone else to take care of a problem like this. So one afternoon, there we both were: me in blue latex gloves with surgical scissors I'd obtained from the medic, and a nervous goat tied to a tree. It was quite a sight: a dodgy captain, who incidentally was running the combat team at the time, trimming the arse hair of a goat at the front of his headquarters.

A couple of days later, one of the smaller infantry soldiers, perhaps with a complex about his height, told me that he killed goats at home as a pastime. Obviously I didn't sound interested enough, so he then told me that he planned to kill our goat. I was suitably impressed – though in the end he never touched her.

13

SOLDIER 17

LATE JUNE BROUGHT A NEW DEVELOPMENT. The board of inquiry continued to call witnesses, who were allocated numbers in an attempt at anonymity. Soldier 17 was a sleepy-looking, lazy little man, continually being caught doing the wrong thing. He had been one of the two blokes in the room when Jake shot himself. In a twist of fate, neither soldier had been facing Jake. As a result, they could offer nothing but speculation and conjecture on how he had managed to get shot.

Soldier 17, in the limelight of the inquiry, decided it was his obligation to tell the board that our equipment was 'all fucked'. He also thought it necessary to canvas every wild theory about how Jake had died.

As an officer, it's your job to look after your soldiers always. Even when you have to discipline them after they break the rules, it has to be fair and in the interests of turning the situation around so that it never happens again. But we all struggled with Soldier 17. Knowing he was going to the inquiry and telling blatant lies about how we operated made us detest him. But we couldn't show it. Our hope was that his claims would be called into question by the board and he would face disciplinary action for his fabrications. But he was never held to account for what he said, nor for the confusion and doubt he brought to the case. Nor for dragging the name of the entire combat team, all 110 of us, through the mud.

The facts themselves were crazy enough, without Soldier 17 adding his fanciful speculation on what may have occurred. I never understood why this young man – who had the board of inquiry listening to him and who therefore could have helped the situation – instead chose to roll grenades into the room with his stories, lies and ill-conceived speculation.

*

News broke that Abu Musab al-Zarqawi had been killed in a fire-fight up in Baqubah, one of the towns we drove through on our way to Kirkush. Not long after the attack in 2004, Zarqawi had claimed responsibility for the bomb that injured me. He had it coming. I didn't feel anything, except maybe a touch sad that one more person was dead. But if it was he who conducted the televised beheadings, well, you can't excuse that. Those were the acts of an evil man.

*

During all this, in early July I went on two weeks' leave with my beautiful wife, riding scooters around Tuscany, drinking wine in picturesque seaside piazzas and just getting to know each other again.

It was such a shift from Baghdad, from having to be alert at all times, having to give the men the impression that you were always confident, ready to manage an emergency, a bomb going off, a rocket siren, a shooting. Italy was a universe away from all that.

We slept in, walked all morning, lunched on enormous bowls of pasta, went on short boat trips along the coast, and had ice-cream in the afternoons.

We hired a scooter and went exploring with no real plan. Outside Sienna, we stumbled on a horse race. It was in a paddock by the roadside and we would not have noticed it had it not been for the crowds of locals sitting on fences and watching as the horses thundered by on the uneven hill track and the race caller chattered in Italian. Nobody noticed or cared when we parked the scooter and found ourselves a patch of grass on which to sit together and watch.

No-one would have guessed that we were a couple who had been separated on other sides of the world, me in a war zone, Crystal nervous back in Australia, trying to live her life but missing me and being frightened every time the phone rang.

We would have just looked like any young couple in love.

*

When I returned, I discovered that one of the senior non-commissioned officers had gone home. It was explained to me on my way in from Kuwait in hushed tones: 'Oh and Warrant Officer ——'s gone.'

'Why?' I asked.

'Psych.'

He was an older man with a neo-Nazi persona, tattoos and constant deadpan expression. He always made out that he was an old-school soldier – hard living, hard discipline, no compromise. The sort of man I thought had been bred out of the army by the mid-2000s. My belief was that the persona was just a cover to hide his shortcomings. In the end I was proved right. Although it had been effective in gaining the admiration and respect of some of the soldiers, others just found him strange.

Back in Australia during the lead-up training, I had found him wanting in a lot of key areas. I believed he was completely in over his head working with a group like SECDET – a combat team made of a mix of skills and corps. He claimed to be fiercely devoted to the infantry, so much so he was unable to work with other corps.

While many of our non-commissioned officers and warrant officers were extremely hardworking and professional, this NCO struggled with relatively simple administrative tasks, and the more we dug, the more we found that many people had covered for him.

Things became really poisonous when he was chosen by the Boss to go back to Australia after Jake was killed. After a few days, stories came back to us that he had been hinting to everybody he met that the Boss 'wasn't handling things well'. He had been saying it was lucky he had been there personally to hold the combat team together.

Then we learnt that in the lead-up to the board of inquiry he had been trying to coerce some of the soldiers into saying certain things: 'Just change your story a little . . .'; 'Just draw some of the attention away from us.' The Boss got wind of this and quickly stamped it out. There had been enough unfounded accusations of cover-ups without someone getting impressionable young soldiers to give false statements.

Interestingly and worryingly, when these soldiers were asked to write statements about what had been said between them and the warrant officer, they all refused, claiming they couldn't recall details. So he still had a concerning amount of influence within the combat team.

While I was away on leave, the Boss counselled him again and again. No improvement. The Boss took action to sack him – to show significant evidence that he was unsuitable for the job he was doing, and then send him back to Australia. All the arrangements were made. The Boss told him a determination would be made on him. The day he was going to tell him he was going home – wham . . . 'I have dreams of shooting myself . . . and others,' he said. The psychs were informed and he was quickly flown out of Iraq and back to Australia.

This was his way of saving face when he had been shown up

as not capable of doing the job under pressure. It was the easy way of going home – keeping allowances and medals, and some credibility. He had been involved enough with Jake's repatriation that no-one could question the authenticity of his mental-health issue. But we knew the truth.

What disgusted me most was that many people have worked so hard over many years to remove the stigma of mental-health issues within Defence, but this individual embodied all the stereotypes about malingering and using mental health as an excuse and an easy way out.

*

The board of inquiry continued through August. It was frustrating. Rather than listening to the facts, people were listening to the lies of a disgruntled digger, who, for the first and hopefully last time in his life, had a captive audience. I was very disenchanted with the Defence hierarchy and angry with the media.

Soldier 17 told the board that we all regularly failed to clear our pistols, we swung them on our fingers 'Wild West' style, it was 54 degrees every day, and we were shot at every day. He was telling lies, but the real tragedy was that he was getting away with it, and, worse still, people were listening to him.

The media was having a field day and we were feeling forgotten. There seemed to be no acknowledgment that we were in Baghdad and doing a dangerous, difficult job. The biggest problem was what the stories – including the claim that we had somehow conspired to kill Jake – bouncing around the media did to morale. Jake's mum, like any good mother, could not see how her son might have been at fault. Soldier 17's lies added fuel to her theories.

There was DNA on Jake's pistol that wasn't his. To us in SECDET, that was completely understandable: it was probably the case with every one of our weapons. Handing it in and out of the armoury, assisting a friend to clean their weapon – there were countless reasonable explanations as to how someone's DNA could get on someone else's weapon. But this further stoked the conspiracy theories.

We were all asked to give DNA samples. One of the police would do a quick mouth swab and that was that. A handful of soldiers refused – we couldn't force them. I was puzzled by their attitude. They were all told that the samples could not be used for any other purpose than the investigation, and that following it they would be destroyed. None of those who refused were involved in the investigation, nor were they even in Jake's platoon. They could not possibly have had anything to do with the incident. We exchanged ideas on why they had refused. For one of the guys who was older than the rest and had led a fairly wild life, we speculated that he feared a DNA sample would confirm he had fathered children he did not want to be associated with. As for the others – I didn't know. Maybe they were conspiracy theorists themselves, who did not believe that the results would be destroyed at the conclusion of the investigation.

Maybe they felt that these samples were all fed into a 'Big Brother' database to keep tabs on us.

Maybe they were just sick of the investigation.

*

Meanwhile, the Australian embassy continued on with its work, and we continued escorting officials to their diplomatic meetings.

Our bodyguards lived in the back pockets of the diplomats, day in, day out. In some ways I felt sorry for the diplomatic staff: while our deployments were six months, they would do eighteen months or even longer depending on their level of seniority. While we got out and saw some of the country, they generally saw only the few square kilometres of the International Zone. When they left it, they travelled in the dark in the back of our vehicles until we could drop them and their bodyguards in the compound or as close to it as possible. Theirs was a siege mentality. The embassy, in the heart of the International Zone, was pretty much their world.

One warm evening, the ambassador invited the SECDET hierarchy to join him for crab gumbo on the embassy lawn. An American friend had offered to make gumbo, and they had decided to make an occasion of it. The seafood was obtained through various means and a huge pot greeted us in the kitchen when we arrived. Several of the embassy staff had been drinking heavily, and they greeted us warmly as we made our way out onto the grass.

The consul general, a DFAT veteran, sat next to me. He was a known drinker, who was constantly picked up from boozy evenings at the UK embassy and other venues. He started to speak in a slurred voice. He asked me about my previous time in Baghdad and the IED incident that had led to my premature return to Australia. After a couple of minutes of chatting, his tone suddenly became aggressive and he accused me of a being a 'bloody fool'. He said that as I'd almost been killed the first time, I was an idiot to return to Iraq. I gritted my teeth and took the insults. While he might have been right in some respects, it was also a bit rich – I was the second-in-command of the combat team specifically assigned to protect him.

*

In mid-August the Boss came back from another session in front of the board of inquiry. When he returned to the Cove, he was strangely relaxed. They had obviously roasted him. Maybe he had not had enough sleep.

He explained to me some of the ridiculous questions he had been asked, such as 'Why did you move the body?' He had to explain that in this circumstance, as Jake had a pulse, he was not considered a 'body', but rather a casualty that required hospitalisation.

I tried to take the pressure off him where possible, as so much of his time was consumed by the inquiry and managing the constant flow of questions from Australia and the headquarters at Camp Victory. In some ways it was professionally very rewarding for me, as I got to oversee most aspects of the day-to-day running of the combat team. This was much more responsibility than your average junior Captain ever takes on.

But even so, events must have been taking a colossal personal toll on the Boss. He had a phone in his accommodation that rang all hours of the night during the working day in Australia. None of the calls was urgent; the callers could have sent emails, or stayed late at work until morning in Baghdad and made the call then. But staff officers were filled with a sense of their own importance or the importance of the general they worked for. No-one could wait – they needed an answer now.

So the Boss fended off calls all through the night.

He had his character called into question. The media was accusing him of orchestrating a cover-up. Jake's mother was accusing him of lying.

He had the combat team's procedure for weapons-handling called into question, a policy that we had inherited from our predecessors, but which the Boss had insisted we rewrite to ensure it was appropriate and robust. We had spent days reviewing and rewriting this procedure before arriving in Baghdad, then nights when we first arrived ensuring it was current and the soldiers understood it. This seemed to be completely overlooked by the board.

The Boss confided in me that the brigadier had told him that his career would likely suffer, even if the board found no systemic issues or leadership problems. The Boss was then a senior major and waiting for confirmation that he had been selected for Command and Staff College the following year, which was the next career milestone. The brigadier had implied there was a good chance he would not be panelled on the course and his career would stall.

There seemed little acknowledgment that he had a combat team to run in the most dangerous city on the planet. Somehow, commanding 110 soldiers and officers played second fiddle to fronting the board of inquiry.

And that bloody phone kept on ringing through the night, ensuring the Boss never got more than a couple of hours' sleep and that his mind was always buzzing. I could hear it ringing from my room. One day I went and unplugged it when he was out. It took him a couple of days to realise. He questioned me and I was immediately up-front. Yes, I had unplugged it; if they really wanted him, they could call the command post phone. He gave me a smirk that could have meant anything, and we never spoke of it again.

*

We hadn't had another weapons incident since Jake was killed, not until the very day the board of inquiry asked the Boss whether these were repeated events. Then one of the boys had a 'negligent discharge' with his pistol – a classic case of someone fucking up and not thinking when he was going through his drills. He had accidentally left the magazine on when he went to clear the pistol, and when he released the working parts and fired the action, he fired off a round – straight into the unload bay, an open drum full of sand, specifically designed and placed to catch bullets if such mistakes are made.

It was another mishap – a mistake that seemed to coincide with and exacerbate other problems. This almost seemed to be a theme of our time in Baghdad.

With one of the gunners, Scotty, in front of the Victory Arch (Crossed Swords) monument.

Loading one of the Phase 3 ASLAVs for transport to Iraq.

ASLAVs departing the Flats through the Hesco chicane.

Al-Faw Palace, Baghdad.

View from the Flats to the north-east.

The same view moments after the IED detonated. The still image is captured from the footage taken by the Australian snipers on the roof of the Flats.

My vehicle sustained significant damage in the IED blast.

The house that was adjacent to the IED blast.

An Iraqi fire-fighter hoses blood from the footpath after the blast.

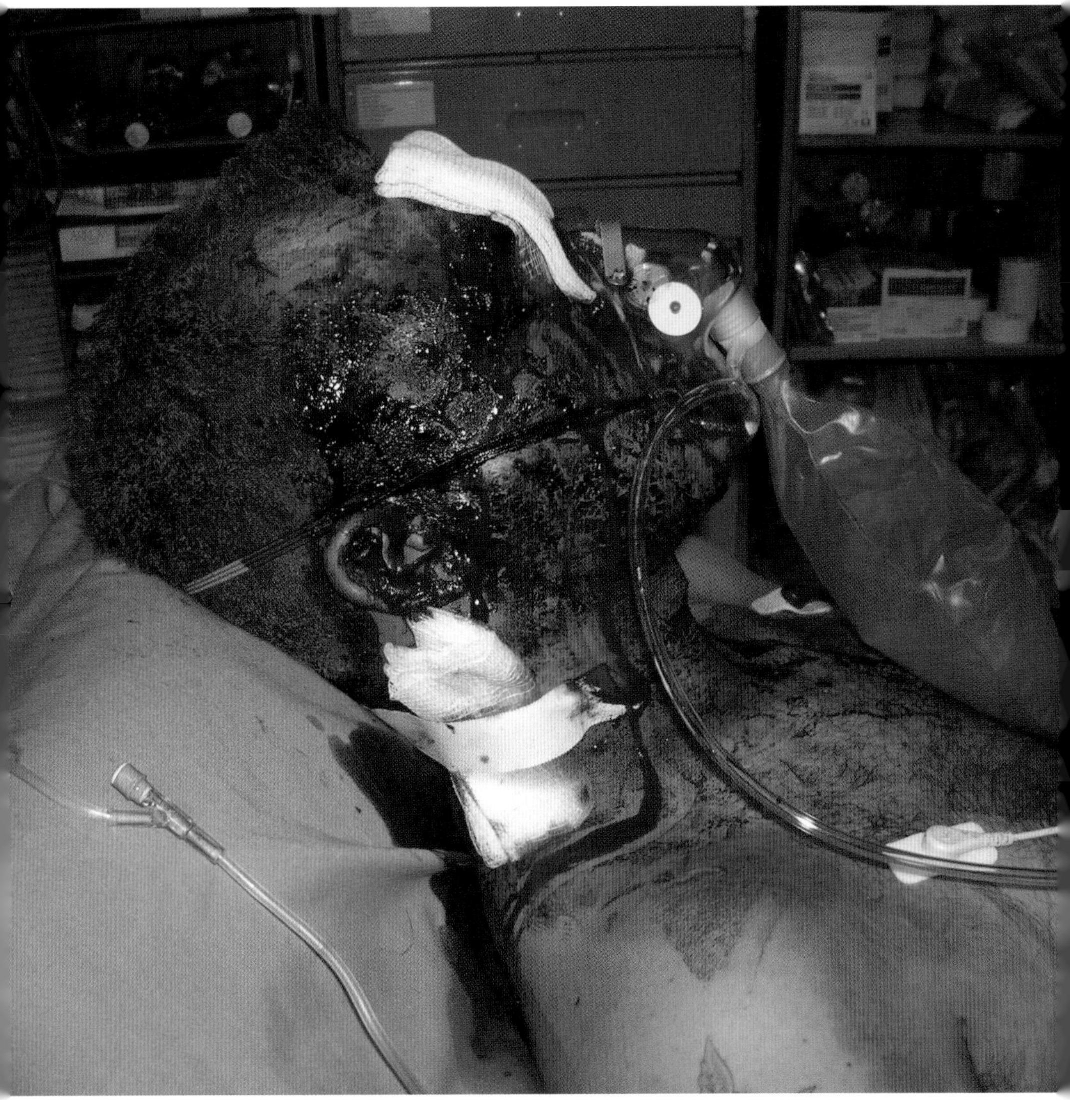

At the CSH, Baghdad, following the IED strike.

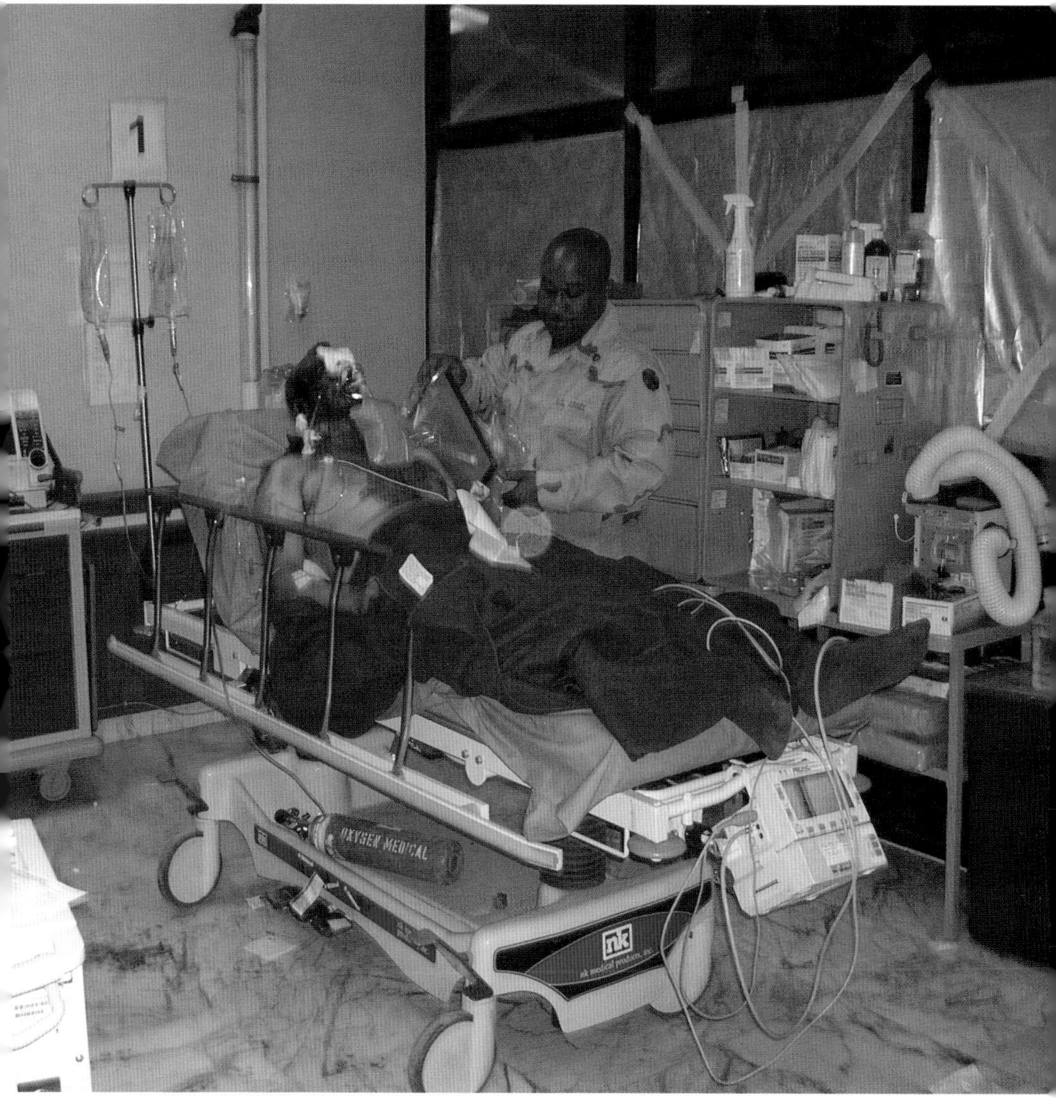
1
OXYGEN MEDICAL
nk

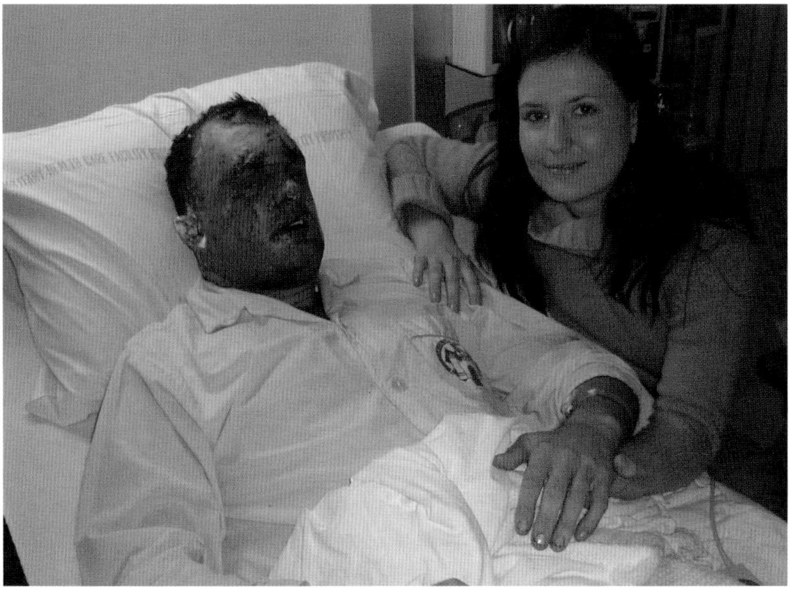

Crystal with me in Germany.

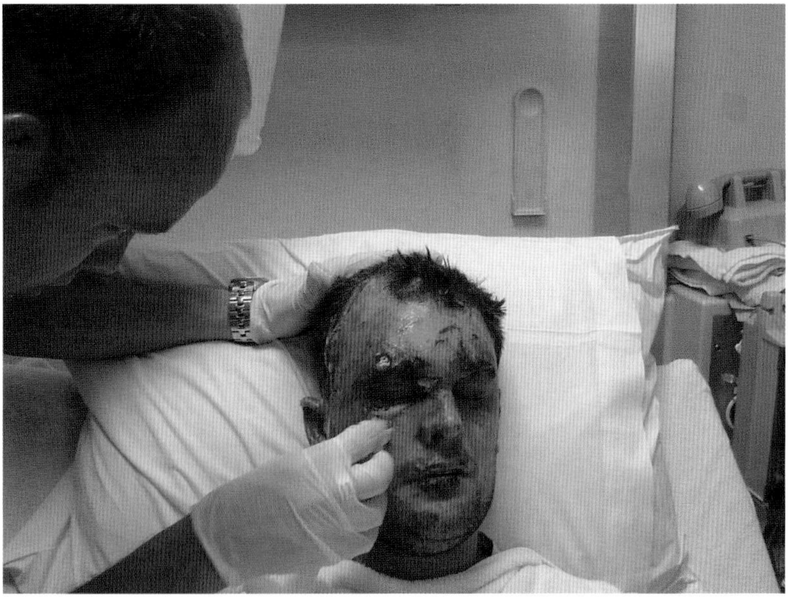

Getting cleaned up – the two holes where the fragmentation had penetrated my sinus cavity beside and above my right eye were packed with wadding.

My boots, now held by the Australian War Memorial
(photo courtesy of the AWM).

The Cove, with the former Ba'ath Party Headquarters in the background.

SECDET IX soldier (photo courtesy of Jim Culloden).

Memorial plaque for Private Jacob Kovco.

Anzac Day in Baghdad, 2006.

With the Boss on Anzac Day, out the front of the SECDET headquarters.

The impact site where the rocket hit the T-wall.

The damaged Hilux: incredibly none of the eight occupants was seriously injured.

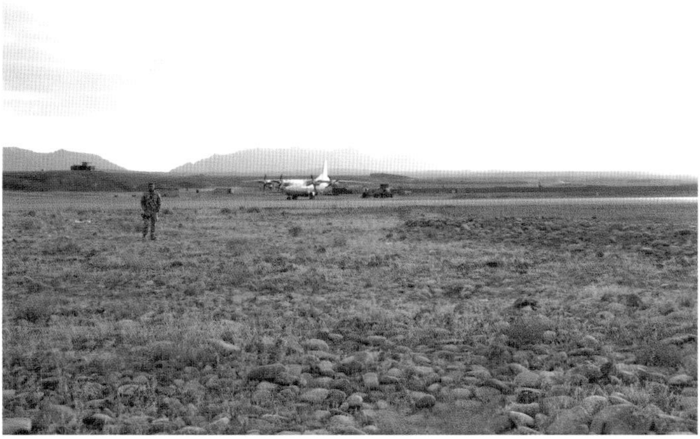

Looking for the impact site of a rocket attack on the airfield from the previous night.

Mortar rounds lashed together with rubber inner tube – a common main charge throughout the province.

The blokes at a strike near Patrol Base Mashal – Pete is in the crater.

My squadron at Shoalwater Bay Military Training Area in mid-2012.

The team outside our lab and office in Tarin Kowt.

Four days after my return from Afghanistan, little Zoe was born.

Ten years to the day since the IED attack in Baghdad: at Admiralty House, Sydney, with my old troop. Matt is fourth from the right.

14

ESCALATION OF FORCE

KAYS JUMA, AN IRAQI-BORN AUSTRALIAN, was a professor of agriculture who spent half his life in Adelaide and the other half in Baghdad. He worked at the university and lived only a few hundred metres down the road, on the Karadah Peninsula. In his seventies, he travelled with his elderly Australian wife, Barbara. He was planning on retiring in a few weeks and returning to Adelaide permanently.

One afternoon, he told his wife that he was going to the shops to get some milk and eggs. No-one knows why, but on approaching the 14 July checkpoint at the bridge over the Tigris, he didn't stop for the banked-up traffic. In a city where everyone lived in fear of suicide vehicles, he continued to drive towards the private security vehicles. He didn't stop. The security contractors claimed they flashed headlights, shouted, fired flares, and pointed weapons, but he only stopped when they shot him. It was a classic 'escalation of force' incident.

He died on the way to the Coalition hospital in the International Zone, the same hospital they had taken me to. Our blokes saw him being brought in in a civilian van. Nothing could be done.

By all accounts, it was an Australian security contractor who shot him. The company denied it, but they were probably protecting their own.

Another surreal and awful event: an elderly man, who had dual Australian and Iraqi citizenship and an Australian wife, shot dead in Baghdad, by an Australian.

Barbara Juma was left widowed in Baghdad; her three sons were back in Australia. 'He was only going to get milk and eggs,' she said when, three days later, we went to pick her up to take her to the airport.

That morning, three ASLAVS rolled out down to the end of the peninsula, where they stopped at a modest house with an elderly woman standing out the front with her suitcases. She had been told to expect army vehicles, but maybe she hadn't expected ASLAVs.

A small, frail lady, Barbara Juma was helped into the back of one of the vehicles with her suitcases before we drove her out to Bagdad International for the flight back to Australia.

'He was only going to get milk and eggs,' she kept saying.

*

A few days after this, one of our patrols shot up a car, killing a man and badly injuring three others. They did exactly what they should have, but it was all over the Iraqi press.

It was getting late in the afternoon, and a reconnaissance of the Iraqi Ministry of Trade was complete and our vehicles were leaving to return to the International Zone. Traffic was banked up at the ministry checkpoints as the ASLAV patrol rolled out of the main gates onto the main road.

As the ASLAV patrol passed through the gates of the ministry, a white four-wheel drive broke from a checkpoint. It accelerated towards the patrol, then swerved between the ASLAVs, and the boys opened fire, assuming it was a suicide vehicle.

They got back all geed up with adrenaline. I sat them down to put together the incident report. As we drew up a diagram of the ministry and the surrounding streets on the large conference table, they excitedly talked me through what they recalled.

Some thought they had been shot at from the car; others weren't sure. Either way, it was clear that they had taken the correct steps before they engaged a vehicle that showed every sign of being a suicide IED. Even so, something about the incident didn't smell right – they told me that there was more than one person in the car and that there was no detonation, although it had come close enough to do real damage.

In the compound, they showed me the ASLAVs. One soldier pointed out some bullet holes in the sandbag around one of the hatches. He thought it was confirmation that they had been shot at from the car. It took only a glance to see something was wrong. The bullets had torn through the sandbags from the wrong side – they were bullet strikes from the ASLAV operator's side.

The adrenaline and euphoria wore off quickly when reports of dead security guards reached us. Many of the men fell into dejection. The ambassador received venomous phone calls from the irate Iraqi trade minister. Like most Iraqi government officials, he employed his extended family as security. The people in the car had been his nephews, who worked as his guards. One was killed, the other three badly wounded; later came reports of a wounded civilian who had been caught in the gunfire.

Three soldiers had opened fire.

The first took it in his stride. He knew he'd acted according to his rules of engagement, and he also knew the Iraqi guards had fucked up. There didn't seem to be any further emotional or ethical issues for him.

The second grappled with the morality of it all for several days, until he spoke to his father. His father said he had seen the news and the pictures of the four-wheel drive with its bullet-riddled windscreen. His comment to his son was 'Nice group', referring to the tight spread of bullet holes in the vehicle's windscreen. With that, the soldier settled.

The third, a real character and, unbeknown to most of us, a deeply religious man, struggled with what he had done. He felt that as he had killed an innocent man, he would now go to hell. It took several visits from the padre and the psychologists to get him in a reasonable mindset.

Tragically, Jamie, the third soldier, died in a motorcycle accident not long after returning to Australia.

*

By August we were starting to plan our return to Australia and the handover with the next combat team. I travelled by ASLAV down Route Irish to the Australian headquarters at Camp Victory. I was there to attend a planning conference for our 'relief in place'.

I found my bed and went to sleep in the happy knowledge that the conference didn't start until 1100 hours, and that not many people knew I was there. So I was surprised to be woken at 0635 hours, when someone entered the dormitory room and came to my bed. He asked, 'Captain Callender? Can you get up and come downstairs?' I dressed and moved out to the hall, to hear two men speaking about someone with a broken leg. In the operations room, a crowd had gathered.

'A rocket has hit the accommodation at SECDET, there are five in hospital.'

I was no help to anyone stuck out at Camp Victory, and I knew of a corporal about to get on a helicopter to fly into the International Zone. She didn't really need that flight. Through one of the staff officers, I convinced the operations staff to let me take her seat. At Landing Zone Washington I found an ASLAV waiting for me. The operator quickly explained what was going on and we headed back to the Cove. I ran the last 200 metres, as I knew the crew would take longer than me to get the ASLAV in as they had to clear all the vehicle's weapons.

I entered the main gates to see that a heavy T-wall positioned to protect the accommodation had been blown almost in half, with the steel reinforcements sticking out and twisted at odd angles. Most of the up-armoured and soft fleet had been damaged, with at least two vehicles completely destroyed. The place buzzed with activity, with sergeants running work parties clearing rubble, removing what was left of the T-wall and the damaged brick wall behind it, and cleaning out the damaged rooms.

At the command post, the cavalry lieutenant was drafting the incident report; the Boss was calmly giving directions. Most of the windows in the building had been blown out, so there was the odd sensation of a cross-breeze where there was usually none.

One accommodation room had been hit, but only by the percussion of the rocket blast, not by the actual fragmentation. The rocket had hit the T-wall first. Thank fuck – otherwise we would have had at least one dead, maybe four.

The two unarmoured GMC Suburbans were cut to pieces. The other armoured SUVs all had holes here and there, their chassis warped by the blast.

The female signals corporal who worked in the 'vault' was by far the worst injured. She had been sleeping on the top bunk, closest to where the rocket hit. She was thrown off her bunk and over a set of lockers and had landed on the floor. The impact had dislocated her hip, fractured her kneecap, split her forehead open and chipped her skull. First reports were of an 'open fracture of the skull', which made me envisage horrific injuries. As it turned out, she was badly injured, but it was not life-threatening. She was evacuated to Germany before getting back to Australia.

The rest of the team suffered mainly cuts, bruises, scratches and grazes. We had been really lucky. When we had arrived in March, besides some useless 'duck and cover' bunkers, the Cove was in no way set up to deal with the constant threat of indirect fire. So we had come up with a plan to harden our defences against rocket attack, which involved surrounding all the structures in the Cove with 7- or 9-foot T-walls of good-quality reinforced concrete.

The plan was approved, and several weeks and almost one hundred thousand dollars later, a team of Iraqi labourers was escorted into the compound to install the walls. One of the lieutenants took charge of the job, and the jokes started about him getting a second platoon, this one made up of 'Smooftys', as the locals were affectionately called.

Safety became a concern when we realised that the sole task of one of the Iraqi team members was to use buckets and tubs to catch the hydraulic fluid that poured from the 20-tonne crane as it moved the T-walls. He would then take this fluid and pour it back into the reservoir, as the crane continued the task. We were also a little frightened by the sight of the frayed and twisted steel cable, which strained and creaked under load.

The T-walls had been installed only three weeks before the rocket strike. For the first time in my life, I had had a direct influence on saving someone's life. It felt good.

Later that day, the brigadier came out to see the injured and inspect the impact site. Several rooms had had their doors blown off, including the Boss's. As they were about to enter the Boss's room, the goat bounded out, looking startled and chewing on a yellow rubber glove. It stopped to stare at them.

'CSM – get this fucking goat out of here!'

15

AFTERMATH

I STAYED A FEW EXTRA DAYS IN BAGHDAD AS part of the handover, providing final guidance to the incoming combat team as they settled in, and also making sure the goat went to a good home – one of the local contractor's daughters had taken a liking to her. I met up with the rest of the combat team in Kuwait for the return trip.

After days of travelling, the Boss, the CSM and I led the procession of soldiers, all in uniform, through customs at Sydney airport and along the walkway to exit to the public area. Cameras flashed and people jostled to get a look at the soldiers the newspapers had written so much about and whose actions had been placed under so much scrutiny.

The Boss's infant daughter broke from the crowd and ran forward crying, 'Da-da, Da-da', and the high-ranking greeting party and reporters swarmed around him and his family. The Boss, ever the consummate professional, stayed for some time answering questions and speaking with generals, before going home to try to resume a normal life.

I travelled on to Brisbane, where I was reunited with my beautiful wife.

*

I always felt the Boss hadn't been looked after. He'd taken things so personally.

The Defence leadership never stepped in to give him proper support. They never said to the media, the government or the board of inquiry, 'Back off, he's commanding 110 soldiers in Baghdad at the height of an insurgency.' Rather, they let the media run their stories uncorrected, let the board of inquiry drag him into headquarters for 3 a.m. grillings, and then told him that his career would suffer.

He never seemed too shaken by it. He always had a smile and an encouraging word or personal question for the soldiers. He always did his best to look after me and the other officers. When we got back to Australia and his commanding officer ordered him to take all his leave before being posted to Canberra, he didn't complain. But it meant he went from the chaos of Baghdad to the silence of his home almost overnight, where he stayed for almost four months before starting his new job.

He also found that when he got home, his wife had no interest in talking about the deployment. She wasn't interested in hearing anything from the previous six months of his life that he had given so much of himself to, and that had taken so much. Eventually his marriage fell to pieces – her silence had masked the fact she was having a long-term affair with another staff officer.

As it turned out, his career didn't suffer, at least not at first. He held a staff position in army headquarters, working for a general for a year, and then attended Command and Staff College in the following year, where he got the second-top position on the course. It was only at the end of our second year back that he was diagnosed with post-traumatic stress. He had called his estranged wife and explained to her that he was pondering the course of his life and questioning why he should still be alive. He had his hunting rifle in his hands when he rang.

He spent weeks in hospital for his psychotic condition, but was released after the drugs and counselling levelled him out. His condition meant that he couldn't continue to serve in the military, so he was discharged not long after being promoted to lieutenant colonel.

On being discharged, he moved to Geelong to be close to his daughters. He lives a much quieter life. With the PTSD he has good weeks and bad. When not dealing with his own demons, he spends a lot of his time helping other troubled veterans.

He's always got his phone handy. He takes a lot of calls from former soldiers. He spends too much of his time convincing them not to take their own life.

PART III: AFGHANISTAN 2009–10

16

A JOB I COULDN'T SAY NO TO

THIS TIME CRYSTAL DECIDED SOMETHING was very wrong. I'd been so quiet; I'd hardly spoken to her in a week. Was I having an affair? Did I not love her anymore? Did I want a divorce? . . .

The truth was I was deploying again, this time for eight months – and I had no idea how to tell her. I thought I needed to be smart about it, to wait for the exact right moment. But in my typical foolish way I got it all wrong.

The army only deploys volunteers, but most go when their unit does. Not me this time. I asked to go. I had found a job I knew was right for me. I like to think that it was the only job I would ever have volunteered for. We had a daughter now. Little Eva made things very different. I felt older, more mature, and I was not interested in chasing adventures or settling scores. This time it was the *role* I couldn't turn down. It was a chance to save lives, or at the very least put things in place that would save lives, and not just those of other soldiers – civilians were getting maimed and killed too.

How could I not volunteer? It was an opportunity to help stop use of the very same weapons that had injured me and killed so many. So I didn't say no; in fact I put myself forward, knowing all the while that Crystal would be devastated. I hoped that although we would suffer a little by being separated, this would be outweighed by helping to save lives or at least slow the spread of the technology and techniques used in the bombs.

When I told her, Crystal didn't break plates in the backyard – she just cried and cried and was really angry with me. And I deserved it. I would be training in Townsville, away from home for three months, with the battle-group that I would support on an eight-month deployment. All up I would be away for about a year.

*

After returning from Iraq, I had spent time with the Recruit Training Battalion in Wagga Wagga, trying to be optimistic about a posting that seemed like a waste because I achieved very little. During the year in Wagga, my personal life took precedence over my career when we found out that Crystal was pregnant, and then, about halfway through the pregnancy, that the child, Jack, had a serious congenital disorder. In the end, Jack was delivered stillborn at twenty-one weeks. Our lives were turned upside-down. For all I had been through, and will go through, I hope never again to experience anything as painful as losing a child.

My posting to Wagga Wagga was cut from two years to one around the time we found out Crystal was pregnant again. In late 2007 we moved to Canberra so that I could commence work with the Counter-IED Taskforce in Russell Offices.

We were both very nervous about this second pregnancy, but not long after we moved to Canberra, Crystal gave birth to a healthy little girl: my beautiful daughter Eva. I would work in an office, be home each night at a reasonable hour, and I definitely did not expect to be deployed to war zones. The new posting was the perfect job for a new dad.

Since 2006, when I had first heard about it, I had been working hard to be assigned to the taskforce. Throughout 2006 and 2007 I had conducted an underhand campaign of lobbying and pestering. I introduced myself to some of the lieutenant colonels at the taskforce, who in turn introduced me to the brigadier who commanded the team. Together we circumvented the normal process and I was asked for specifically for the role.

The taskforce had been created to provide strategic oversight and direction for the entire defence force's efforts against improvised explosive devices. As part of my role, I was introduced to the upper echelons of Defence, and while I spent far too much time in formal uniform and behind a desk, I also sank my teeth into the job and enjoyed it. I was thrust into a world where I regularly briefed generals, cabinet ministers, police, scientists and intelligence specialists.

It was a time of extremes: one day I would be making sure enough lunches had been ordered for a course we were running, and the next I would be briefing the Chief of Army on the latest, highly sensitive, counter-IED initiatives and technology. My head spun for the first three months, and I spent the remainder of my time there in a state of mild confusion.

The taskforce was a mix of military and civilians – dedicated and handpicked individuals who devoted their time to understanding IEDs and looking for ways to combat them. From them, I learnt about the value of thorough intelligence processes to identify current and emerging threats and perpetrators.

Before this, my understanding had been focused on physical protection: body armour, ballistic goggles, helmets and vehicles to protect against blast and fragmentation; anti-flash hoods and gloves to protect against the extreme heat generated in an explosion; jammers to stop radio-controlled bombs from detonating.

Now I was introduced to the idea of technical intelligence by my new boss, an extremely devoted lieutenant colonel, who was single, in his late thirties and had a work ethic I have encountered in only a few. I found him one morning at his desk in the same clothes he had been wearing the evening before. 'Did you make it home last night, sir?' I asked. His mumbled reply about having a lot of high-priority jobs on his plate and the half-eaten chocolate cake in the fridge answered my question. We would joke about buying him a dog to give him a reason to go home.

Another character in our team was an ammunition technical officer with, it seemed, three brains. He broadened my understanding of technical intelligence and what a weapons intelligence team deployed in theatre could achieve. He had received several commendations from Australia and the United States for his work running one such team for Taskforce Troy, the US Counter-IED Taskforce in Iraq. He showed me how much information and 'actionable intelligence' could be derived from incident sites.

Technical intelligence involves understanding everything about an incident: what the good guys were doing; what the bad guys were trying to achieve; how the IED was emplaced; what it was made up of; the triggering method; the chemical make-up of the explosive charge; the power supply; how it was all connected; whether fingerprints or DNA had been left during the fabrication or emplacing . . . the list goes on. If you take all this information and compare it with other IED incidents, you start to see patterns, trends and signatures that provide clues as to who built it, who emplaced it, and what the supply chain looked like. Then you overlay all the other intelligence that you have about insurgents, and suddenly real information starts to fall out.

There are two valuable outcomes from this. First, you have information about attacks that you can feed to soldiers so they understand the bombs being used against them. Understanding the weapons allows them to train and develop tactics to protect themselves. Second, a 'target pack' can be built with all the information, so that an individual bombmaker, transporter or trainer can be targeted. This target pack would drive 'cordon and search' operations by joint Coalition and Afghan soldiers or, if you pulled together some really solid information, the Special Forces might even use it for raids to capture key insurgents or in planning more secretive operations.

The taskforce in Canberra stood up the first Australian Weapons Intelligence Team, which deployed to Afghanistan in April 2008. It was designed to work with our deployed units, as well as Dutch, US and UK forces, to gain answers to these questions. I helped to set it up, but did not go myself – in fact, at this early stage I had no desire to be part of one of the teams. Unfortunately, for several reasons this team and the one after it received a frosty reception from the Australian units they were supposed to be supporting. Some of it was due to personalities, some to a complete lack of understanding of what they were doing there (including from the team members themselves), but primarily it was because many commanding officers and staff saw four blokes whose task they did not understand but who were, due to the cap on overall deployment numbers, taking four valuable positions from them – a brick of infantry, or an ASLAV crew.

The team's role was something new and not clearly understood. Also, it was an unusual thing for the Australian military, a bit of a mongrel – four people with different but complementary skills pulled together rather than coming from a regular unit.

The more I learnt about the team, the more I understood how valuable these four people were – they could provide so much more than another brick of infantry or a vehicle crew.

*

It was widely acknowledged that the best person to be the next team leader would be an officer, more specifically an arms corps officer. And so, on a cold morning in mid-2008, I had, as alcoholics call it, a 'moment of clarity' as I ran between the Australian War Memorial and Parliament House on the 9-kilometre route from home to the office. *The best person for the next deployment would be me.*

I never found out exactly what happened; I discussed my idea with only one person, but that very same day the brigadier called me in to say that he wanted me to lead the next team. So it was settled.

My first task was to put together a good crew for the third rotation. Technical intelligence is a discipline that requires specialists. First we needed an explosive ordnance disposal (EOD) technician, someone with a detailed understanding of explosives. On my team this was Pete, a very experienced air-force flight sergeant, a man who had joined the military in his late teens as an apprentice avionic technician and later shifted to EOD. He was highly intelligent, with a very precise view on explosives and a driven curiosity about the electronics behind the emerging IED technologies. His enthusiasm, mixed with his amicable nature, ensured I could always rely on him to get people on side.

Being air force also meant that Pete did not come from the same mould as his army peers, who were generally gruff and harder to work with. Importantly, he shared my views on how the team should run and what we needed to do. Like me, he had a young family whom he didn't like spending time away from, but he knew this job was important – important enough to leave his wife and young boys for nearly a year. Due to his character and senior non-commissioned rank, he was the obvious choice to be the second-in-command of the team.

Next was the investigator, or 'scenes of crime officer', who brought an understanding of forensic recovery, biometrics and evidence preservation. I struggled to find the right bloke for the job. The defence investigative service had put out a request for an 'expression of interest' and then just sent the first person who applied. But I found I couldn't take him to Afghanistan because, even after months of training, he failed to understand the fundamentals of the job. He put uncovered hands over evidence he was supposed to be preserving, broke the chain of custody of evidence, and failed to show any real understanding of how explosives worked. His replacement wasn't much better and gave me ongoing problems throughout our eight-month tour. But he was a real character, a giant bald fellow with a shiny scalp, and what he lacked in experience and technical know-how, he made up for with enthusiasm. He gave us a lot of good laughs along the way.

My intelligence bloke was exactly the man I needed: a walking database of historic IED events and trends. He could recall the most obscure explosive incident from years earlier. I would take him with me to important meetings so he could back me up with facts while I prattled away. In classic intelligence corps fashion, he didn't fare well out of the office. He needed to eat regularly and would get dizzy, surly and usually just stop talking unless he got enough to eat at three-hour intervals.

Finally, our team of four needed a tactical adviser, the bloke who should understand what the friendly forces were doing at the time of the incident and be able to assess what the enemy was doing or attempting to do. He should be able to liaise with commanders on the ground and speak their language when it came to discussing tactics.

This was me.

*

I constantly grappled with why I was going to Afghanistan. I had a young daughter, a beautiful wife . . . what was I doing? Beau put my problems in perspective.

Beau had been one of my junior crew commanders back in 2004 and we met up again during the training in Townsville. This would be his fourth deployment: three to Iraq, and this was his first to Afghanistan. He was going over as a patrol commander in charge of two or three ASLAVs and a key adviser on how armoured vehicles were best employed.

Beau was a larrikin in the extreme. He was of average height and build, with a shaved head. He spoke in a deliberate manner with a very occasional minor stutter – a trait I have seen in many highly intelligent, considered people.

Beau lived on the fringes of social norms, but not in a bad way – at least, not to my mind. His sense of humour was based purely on filth, and he had his quirks. His running joke was to see how much loose change he could stuff into his foreskin, after which he would jump on a table and let go of his penis so the change fell everywhere. I remember seeing him limping one Monday morning. When I asked him what had happened, he replied that he had tried to break his record and must have pushed in too many 50-cent coins.

He loved KFC . . . but only the chicken skin. He told me he had nearly crashed his car because his hands got so slippery from the grease that he couldn't hold the wheel properly.

His filthy, irreverent jokes, crass behaviour (which usually involved one of his testacles appearing when it shouldn't) and infectious laugh would regularly have us all in hysterics. He was always the one to take things too far.

But that was only one side of Beau. The other was always close to the surface. It was the highly professional soldier: intelligent, enthusiastic and loyal. He mentored and disciplined younger soldiers with ease, and advised and supported his superiors with an authority that belied his age and relatively junior rank.

As a young lance corporal, he was widely acknowledged as the best gunnery instructor in the regiment, a title usually only held by senior warrant officers or the regimental sergeant major.

In the compound, he demanded perfection from the junior soldiers. They looked up to him and hoped that when he switched back to being a larrikin they could be in on his jokes and clowning.

In my eyes, Beau was the quintessential soldier – a man who trained hard to do things that no-one but a soldier gets trained to do: to protect lives and take lives.

In Iraq, it hadn't taken long before Beau had to kill. During the ambush at Tal Afar, after insurgents had sprung the ambush with a salvo of RPGs that somehow missed all the vehicles, Beau cut an insurgent in half with the .50 calibre on the remote weapon station. It was a remote system that had a counterintuitive sighting system, which I thought was damn near impossible to fire accurately on the move. Yet Beau had killed a man with precision while travelling at speed.

We caught up a few times during the Townsville training, although I noticed Beau missed a few days. When he returned, he confided that he and his girlfriend had lost their triplets. In a clinical, yet matter-of-fact way he told me how they had been 'cut out' of his partner.

I had been missing Crystal and questioning my decision to go on my third deployment. Despite the personal tragedy he'd just suffered, Beau was training to go on his fourth. He put things squarely in perspective for me.

Perhaps he was running away from things. Perhaps he was doing what he thought was right. Either way, Beau's commitment to his profession could not be questioned. It was blokes like Beau that I was hoping to protect.

17

TARIN KOWT

SOMEHOW I HAD IT IN MY HEAD THAT WE would fly into a 'superbase' like the ones I had known in Iraq – Balad and Camp Victory. But Tarin Kowt was different. The Hercules dropped sharply, then throttled up to land on the sloping dirt strip. It didn't look like much more than a gravel quarry cut out of the hillside. On the eastern side was a low tower and beyond it was the rest of the base.

On the western side, near a few squat buildings, a handful of helicopters were parked: Kiowa Warriors, small recon airframes that had been converted to light attack helicopters with a couple of Hellfire rockets under each stumpy wing; Apaches, the serious attack helicopters; a couple of Chinooks; and about half a dozen Black Hawks, a few used as medivac helicopters, the rest as transports.

I didn't yet understand how important these helicopters would be for carrying out my job. Neither of the two previous teams had been deployed out to incident sites at short notice. But it wouldn't be long before we had our first task.

My first impression of the base was that it looked as though it had been bought from Ikea. While there were a few older permanent buildings, most were sandy yellow shipping containers, arranged to make a little city. I had heard of the chalets, the buildings made of armoured shipping containers, but I hadn't pictured how the place would look.

They were completely modular. Walls could be removed to make larger rooms. The mess was made of about twenty containers. The accommodation was single containers joined together to make a series of rooms connected by a long hallway. I shared a room with two other officers. We had bunk beds that somehow all jammed into the long narrow space.

I had the bed by the large armoured door that would clunk and groan when anyone came in or out. I got used to it quickly, lucky in that I could sleep through most things, sometimes to my detriment. In Baghdad I had woken some mornings to hear everyone say, 'Wow, that rocket hit close last night.' I had blissfully slept through the whole thing.

We spent our spare time reading the most recent IED reports. Uruzgan province: for such a simple place, it seemed so complex. The provincial government was corrupt and vying for power with a 'shadow' Taliban government. The chief of police was really an illiterate warlord who would extort a fortune from people using the main road from Tarin Kowt to Kandahar.

Only a day before we arrived, one of the local police chiefs had blown himself and his deputy to pieces while trying to disarm a bomb. His trick of pulling at an IED with a hook on a short pole had failed him. It had worked many times before, but this time he inadvertently triggered the device. The boys told me how they watched locals gather remains from the site of the explosion and carry them up the hill to the local graveyard for burial. One man carried severed legs, while another carried a spinal column from which much of the flesh had been blown off. According to their religion, they must be buried before sundown.

The Australian, Dutch, French and US soldiers here trained and mentored Afghan soldiers, who worked out of the main base and about a dozen smaller patrol bases dotted through the surrounding valleys.

Most of the Afghan soldiers had come from the north of the country. They were brought into the province to fight the Taliban and stop the shadow government from coming to power through violence. Being from the north meant they could not be influenced by tribal affiliations, the issue that affected the local police. As in any culture with a strong tribal influence, Afghan allegiances lay first with their family and tribe, then with their profession – for this reason, the local police could not be trusted. But the soldiers did not have this issue. They came from many different tribal groups. While the Hazara, with their eastern Eurasian features, were most obvious, very few of the soldiers in the Afghan army's 4th Brigade, the formation operating within the province, were of the local Pashtu tribal affiliation. The brigade even spoke a different language: Dari. The Dari-speaking soldiers regularly needed interpreters to speak with the Pashtu-speaking locals.

*

In my first week in Tarin Kowt, I volunteered to spend four days commanding a Bushmaster vehicle for a patrol up to Chora and back down through the Baluchi Valley. The route stopped at most of the key bases where Australian teams lived with their Afghan army counterparts.

We were up before dawn on the day we departed. The explosive ordnance disposal (EOD) guys needed a crew commander, so it made sense that I should jump in and take charge of their vehicle. But it had a remote weapon station on it, for which, frustratingly, I was not qualified. Commanding a vehicle with a weapon system you are not qualified to operate is a pretty big no-no. I would be driving around with my finger on the trigger of a weapon system with live rounds. I had used a similar system on the ASLAV, so it wasn't completely foreign, but the only instruction I received, as I sat on the firing point to test-fire the gun before driving out the gate, was, 'Just press that to charge the gun, flick the safety there and fire . . . yep, off you go.' There was no point in making a fuss. I knew enough to be able to shoot when I needed to, and not to loosen off rounds when I didn't.

The long convoy trundled out the back gate of the base towards the centre of Tarin Kowt. The locals watched nervously as the Bushmasters, ASLAVs and armoured trucks chugged past, churning up the dust. It was hot, getting into the peak of summer. Locals stared; some in the centre of town looked down from one of the few two-storey buildings. They talked into mobile phones, likely telling family about a convoy coming through town – either to warn them to stay inside or to inform the local Taliban commanders.

From Tarin Kowt we trundled out into the dasht (the local name for the raw, scorched desert). We followed this to the north-east and up to Chora, where we stopped for the night. We took up a position high on the bald hillside looking down onto the Chora crossing, and then further to the township itself, a small regional centre made up of mudbrick houses, or 'qalas'.

These dwellings sat as they had for many hundreds of years, amid the irrigated greenbelts fed by the river as it wound its way from the higher mountainous country in central Afghanistan. Qalas were compounds surrounded by high walls. They varied in size; some were quite large, with five or six rooms. Many had a main area where the inhabitants cooked over a clay wood-fired stove. Months later, I spent an afternoon in one of these qalas. Besides nearly shooting a dog when it startled us as we attempted to enter a secondary compound, we spent a peaceful few hours during a particularly chaotic time out with a Dutch Marine patrol.

Qalas were designed so that the inhabitants could be almost self-sufficient; they had gardens with small crops, and animals were kept in smaller, adjoining compounds. I was surprised that, even on the hottest days, the mudbrick walls of the houses were cool to touch. They caught the breeze that blew through the valleys and were surprisingly well constructed, many looking like professionally rendered walls you would find back home. I was sure that many in Australia would think these qalas were a little spot of paradise – and would likely pay top dollar for a weekend in such a rustic getaway.

The area was framed by looming, craggy mountain peaks that rose sharply from the river and farming areas. The lush, green, low-lying valleys or 'green zone' contrasted sharply with the dry, dusty dasht and the brutal, jutting mountain ranges.

The next day we pushed on, out past Nyazi and down past Cemetery Hill West, where a couple of Australian snipers and forward observers had nearly been killed about twelve months earlier when the local Taliban had caught them in a hide too far from any support.

About halfway through the valley we stopped the vehicles on the high ground in an overwatch position to support the infantry company as it patrolled down through the green zone. As we sat there baking in the sun, we had a view north-east through the valley, framed by sheer cliffs on either side. Every piece of irrigated land was owned and used by locals. Small plots, usually about a quarter of an acre in size, were used to grow crops all year round: a couple of crops of wheat or corn for food, and a couple of crops of poppies for money.

As we sat in our vehicles, binoculars up, turrets humming, trying to keep track of the infantry, suddenly there came a thump from the north. Even from a distance you could feel the air stiffen. About 2 kilometres up the valley on a dirt road, nothing more than a vehicle track, a cloud of dust and smoke appeared. Soon we got the call on the radio that a civilian vehicle had hit an IED. We packed up and drove to the site.

When we arrived, we learnt it was a family: about eight all up. Two adults and a group of children, ranging from teenagers to small children, were walking along the dirt track up to Chora. Their HiLux had hit an IED, which had detonated under its left front wheel. The explosion had destroyed the front half of the vehicle, but, incredibly, the family had been spared any serious injury. Our medics determined that no-one had sustained any life-threatening injuries – perhaps a few broken ribs, some blood noses, and a few cuts and bruises. The father explained that they were not from the area but a few hours' drive north, so they couldn't rely on the locals for help. They just picked up and started walking home.

It was sickening to consider what might have been if the vehicle had struck the device with its rear wheel or if the explosives had been offset from the trigger, like so many in the area – designed to blow up under the centre of a vehicle.

After the area was cleared, I went forward and recovered what I could of the device. Lollies and small children's trinkets were scattered across the road – the kinds of things Eva would have been playing with. There were also fragments of a yellow palm-oil container used to hold the homemade explosive charge, but not much else.

The road also gave a few tell-tale signs. A line of rocks crossed the track about 10 metres either side of the strike – probably to warn locals. Since the family had been from another part of the province, they had driven past the line, unaware of the bomb waiting in the wheel rut. We will never know for whom it was intended – maybe our convoy, maybe the Afghan police or army.

*

We spent our second night in the dasht out the back of one of the patrol bases – a few huts surrounded by Hesco walls and a few watch-towers where the Afghan soldiers manned machine guns and watched for Taliban attack.

The following day we moved down south towards the Baluchi Pass, where the valley narrows as two mountain ranges converge. The qala walls closed in on either side of the road. A remote weapon station was useless in tight areas like these, so I was constantly up and down from the front seat to the cupola in the centre of the vehicle. When the road got tight, I was up with my rifle on my shoulder, peering over the walls to make sure no-one caught us out by firing an RPG or tossing a grenade from behind a mudbrick wall.

It was hard work. The vehicles were not designed for comfort, and going from the seat to the centre cupola was tricky to do in body armour. I had to reach over and up and heave myself from the seat to a standing position. It was made harder by the need to wear my four-point harness while I was seated, and then untangle myself from it when I stood up.

The seatbelts were important in a strike, to stop you flying around the inside of the vehicle. The force of a blast was enough to kill a man by smashing his head into the roof of the vehicle. When you were in the cupola, a blast was likely to throw you out of the vehicle, but unlikely to kill you. Lower limb injuries were common for crew commanders whose vehicles were hit by IEDs while they were standing in the cupola.

The force of an explosion is something that humans don't generally experience and can't really comprehend – what gases moving at thousands of metres per second will do to an armoured vehicle and its occupants. It was still something that I didn't fully understand myself. Yes, I had been injured by a blast, but my experience of it was limited by my loss of consciousness. I had seen grisly images from US post-mortems of soldiers killed in strikes: photographs and X-rays of crushed necks and heads; spines compressed and driven into brains; soldiers having been pulled from vehicles following a blast appearing almost untouched but stone-cold dead from the acceleration of the vehicle into the air and the inertia that threw them into the roof of the vehicle, breaking their necks and fracturing their skulls.

The blokes in the back showed little sympathy for my contortions as I struggled from the seat to the cupola. On a couple of occasions I was asked if I could stop jumping up and down and just close the cupola hatch so the aircon would work better. Thanks, fuckers.

We stopped when one of the Australian mentors working with the Afghan soldiers spotted two suspicious locals. The Afghan soldiers shot at them and they ran off towards a qala. They vanished in the maze of aqueducts and low walls. A corporal was standing next to the same qala when one of the Afghan soldiers spotted something on the low roof just next to his head. It turned out to be three 82-milimetre mortars, old Russian ones, rigged up with detonating cord and a Russian grenade fuse. It was all ready to go except for a wire to trigger it. By pulling the wire, a small hammer would strike the detonator, which would start the explosive train. The detonating cord would ignite and feed into the noses of the mortars where the explosive fill would be set off, sending the fragmentation from the mortars flying into the air at thousands of metres per second. An ear-splitting crack would shock the air for kilometres around, probably killing anyone standing within 5 metres, and wounding anyone within 100 metres.

Further south, where the valley opened out again into the Tarin Kowt bowl, devices like this were regularly left with the wire tied across a path, or in abandoned buildings. An unsuspecting soldier was likely to trip the device with his foot.

We walked from our vehicles down a steep hillside to the qala where the mortars were found. I packed them in a plastic bag, wearing gloves so as not to contaminate the device with my fingerprints, and we trudged back up the hill to the vehicles.

Those hills were harder to climb than they looked. We were working in an area considerably higher than most places in Australia: 1400 metres or more. With the weight of the mortars in my pack, I was exhausted after the few-hundred-metre climb back to the vehicles, even though I considered myself pretty fit.

We drove back through the dasht the way we came so that we could refuel at Chora, then headed back down to Tarin Kowt. These four days had given me a first glimpse of the countryside and its inhabitants. I had got a taste of the harsh environment the Afghan people lived in. I had seen a young family inexplicably saved from death or maiming. I had started to gain an understanding of what local Afghans endured every day, when a simple trip down one of the dirt tracks linking the population centres could have life-changing – even life-ending – results.

The long hours I spent trundling through the dasht in one of the rear vehicles in the convoy on the return to Tarin Kowt gave me a lot of time to think. I used it to develop a strategy to tackle the challenges I faced in the province. I now had a fair understanding of the environment I was working in, and I was even more convinced that my team had a significant role to play and that we could save lives.

*

Journal entry: *Eva is 1 year and 3 months. I spoke to her and Crystal today. I had the feeling that Eva didn't quite understand who I was – well, what did I expect?*

As I travelled through the Afghan countryside, I was taken by how cute the local children were. We were constantly passing them as our patrol trundled through the built-up areas. It made me miss little Eva even more.

Like I did last time, I had told Crystal I would be spending my time working in a large base behind a desk and not doing anything dangerous. She was pissed at me when I finally called her after getting back – both because I hadn't called her for almost a week and, more importantly, because my cover of a safe desk job had been blown.

But she also had some news to pass on. She was pregnant. Somehow we had timed it perfectly: I had knocked her up in the month before I left. Her due date meant that I should be back in time for the birth. *Should be* . . . it would be close.

More than ever, I felt I had to achieve something in this job: I had to make a difference, have a strategic impact, write reports for everyone from corporals to generals – help save lives. I was buggering up being a husband – leaving Crystal to go through the whole pregnancy alone. So I had to do something right.

18

THE LAB

WORK HAD ALREADY PILED UP BY THE time I got back to the lab. IED components were brought in to us from all over the province by explosives ordnance teams, Dutch, Australian and US patrols, the Afghan army, the Afghan police and various Special Forces units. I was amazed at how inventive the insurgents were in turning junk into deadly devices. We received complete bombs that EOD teams had managed to separate with ropes and hooks: bags full of scraps of yellow plastic, crushed batteries and old Iranian audio wires from bombs that had gone off under vehicles; ingenious anti-tamper switches that had failed to operate; rockets; bullets; RPG rounds; mines; and directional charges designed to explode and shoot forth scrap metal, bullets, nuts and bolts.

Sometimes the Afghan locals would arrive at the front gates with complete IEDs and try to exchange them for money. There were times when these devices were armed and all it would have taken was for someone to press the pressure plate unwittingly and the thing would have gone off.

Our lab was little more than a large room with a table for reverse-engineering the devices, a photographic copy stand, some simple hand tools, an industrial X-ray machine and explosive identification equipment.

We had rooms for storing evidence before it was 'back-loaded' to the more technical labs in Kandahar and Bagram. Another room was our office, where we spent most of our lives, writing reports and trawling through old ones trying to identify trends. Out the back was a shipping container in which we stored any explosives that came back from the field. Every month or so, we would blow up the leftovers on the range at the back of the base. If it was a unique charge, like a shaped charge, or of an unusual chemical make-up, we would send it to Kandahar for testing.

Some days saw a seemingly endless procession of people dropping off remnants of IEDs. A report was written on each one. People were interviewed: where did the IED incident occur? At what time? On what date? Who was involved? Were there casualties? No explosion was an isolated occurrence – there were always links to be made.

The more we understood about the IEDs in the province, the more we could pass on to the people who worked out in the patrol bases: the infantry, artillery forward observers, engineers and armoured corps blokes who spent most of their time 'outside the wire'. The EOD teams would have a better understanding of what they could expect to find and the best ways of 'rendering safe' the devices. Tactics could be developed to minimise the threat.

That all came under the 'force protection' banner. But the real value in what we did was the technical intelligence. This involved identifying trends, grouping incidents through commonalities in fabrication or location, identifying the insurgents we were targeting, and, if we were lucky, linking incidents through fingerprints or DNA found on the recovered components. This required detailed reporting and thorough analysis. It was hard, unglamorous work sifting through old reports, writing new ones and photographing and cataloguing evidence. Nothing sexy, just hard work. But slowly we started to see the trends.

My intelligence analyst was the first to spot one: a road in the Mirabad valley. The past three years had seen a series of strikes and bomb recoveries on a particular short length of dirt road. First the insurgents had used command wire devices, then anti-tamper devices, then radio-controlled IEDs. Looking through the reporting, you could see the bombmaker responsible had the same way of wrapping electrical tape around his battery packs and anti-tamper switches. He targeted Afghan police using the route because they would generally attempt to recover devices – hence the anti-tamper switches. He changed his tactics as new techniques filtered up from Kandahar.

Reports of insurgent IED trainers moving through the Mirabad area matched changes in fabrication and emplacement techniques. Reports of five brothers who were emplacing devices for the Taliban matched the number of footprints and triggerman locations found at sites.

Slowly our picture of the province grew more detailed. In Mirabad, anti-personnel devices targeted police. There were large buried bombs up the Baluchi Valley, with the insurgents in the northern end preferring pressure plates with bare copper wire, and the insurgents halfway up the valley using small anti-personnel mines to trigger their devices. In Deh Rafshan, insurgents used directional devices to target dismounted patrols, and these tactics were followed all the way up to the mouth of the Baluchi Valley.

There were small IED cells operating throughout the province. Some were hard-line Taliban; others emplaced the devices for cash or to prevent scrutiny or reprisal; others just wanted to stay onside with the Taliban because they knew the Coalition forces would not be there forever. Very slowly we started to understand them all.

The biggest problem we had was the quality of the reporting. Because we weren't getting out to sites, we were relying on whoever was on the ground. Through no fault of their own, everyone had a different way of writing a report.

Infantry patrols who were hit in Baluchi reported on tactics – what they were doing; what the insurgents were doing – but they failed to detail anything about the device.

Engineers and EOD guys tended to write very thorough reports about the device but failed to talk much about tactics and regularly just gave us photographs of a hole in the ground and nothing from the surrounding area.

A Dutch public engagement team involved in an attack on a town meeting in Deh Rahwod focused on who was killed and what their affiliations were but failed to talk about either tactics or the device used, even though it was a very unusual motorcycle-borne bomb.

Bushmaster in culvert.

To resolve this problem, we needed to get out to significant incidents. In doing this, we would be breaking new ground. I spent a lot of my time lobbying every commander with a role to play: the person who ran the command post, to ensure we were informed when something happened; the operations officer, to gain permission to go; the aviation liaison officers, to secure seats on helicopters; infantry commanders, so it would not be a surprise when we arrived. I even procured an old truck to get us to the helicopter landing zone in a hurry. For a while I was a man on a mission, and it wasn't long before my bull-headed stubbornness paid off.

*

Tragically, two Australian soldiers were wounded in an IED strike up in the Baluchi Valley. We got the call that they wanted us out there. On landing, we were met by one of the diggers from the patrol at the fringe of the green zone. A Bushmaster sat in the middle of the dirt track with its nose in a large culvert. Its front wheels had both been blown over 100 metres in opposite directions. The casualties, with broken legs and concussion, had been evacuated by the time we arrived.

This was the first time I experienced what I would later realise was one of the strange characteristics of a bomb site. It was as if a hush had fallen over the whole valley. The place was silent except for the subdued sounds of the soldiers as they got on with the administrative tasks that needed to be done to get their patrol moving again. Many settled down quietly in security positions away from the strike site. If it wasn't for the armoured vehicle with its nose in a crater and the two wheel stations with broken and twisted suspension struts sitting 100 metres away on either side of the road, you might not have realised anything was going on.

Pete got the job of looking through the crater. I went and interviewed some of the soldiers involved. Within an hour we were done. We had all the information from the site we needed and the helicopter was inbound. We said our farewells and moved back out of the green and into the hard, baked desert, about 200 metres up a hill behind a small qala to a relatively flat spot where the helicopter could land.

Back at the base in Tarin Kowt, I attended the battle-group nightly brief with General Kelly, commander of all Australian troops in the Middle East, in attendance. I talked through how the incident had occurred and the casualties were sustained. I discussed the device: the size of the charge, and what the trigger was. I gave my assessment of what I thought the insurgents were trying to achieve with the bomb. I detailed all historic incidents that had occurred in the area and on that specific piece of road. Finally, I gave recommendations on how future patrols could minimise the chance of similar attacks.

There were many questions, including several from the general. I would like to think that this was information both he and the battalion commanding officer needed if they were to understand what had happened and inform the command group on how such incidents could be averted in the future.

I also sat in on the 'After Action Review'. When my team's deployment to the site was mentioned, the decision was unanimous – this should be automatic. For incidents where security was in place, we would deploy. I caught a conversation afterwards: 'Why didn't the last battle-group deploy the Weapons Intelligence Team?' to which the reply came, 'Oh, they didn't understand the capability.'

After this we went out to bomb sites regularly. I carried a pager that beeped at me at all times of the day or night. I'd get called in to give advice on what to do with a discovery of explosives or rockets, or to discuss what to do about the Afghan police finding a rocket cache, or to hear how a Dutch patrol had had a bomb go off just near their patrol. Many times we'd reach the battalion command post, a short walk from my lab, and they'd brief me quickly on an incident and tell me a Black Hawk or Chinook was waiting for us. We'd bundle into our clapped-out old truck and be down at the flight line and in the air in minutes, thundering across the rooftops of Tarin Kowt, then out in the dasht before circling over a paddock next to a platoon that had had a strike, or a dirt track where a disabled vehicle sat astride a bomb crater.

Regularly we went out with either Dutch or Australian EOD teams. They would disarm or 'render safe' the IED and we would go in to do the 'exploitation' of the site. Getting helicopters was sometimes difficult. To get around this, we often went out to sites with the Dutch quick reaction force (QRF), a Dutch vehicle patrol that was always waiting to help when another patrol got into trouble – if they'd had a breakdown or hit an IED. It was a running joke that they were really the 'slow reaction force' because nothing happened quickly when you were driving around the province. Often they waited overnight before heading out, because driving the Afghan roads at night was extremely dangerous.

Even so, we organised to have two seats allocated for us with the Dutch QRF. While the Dutch used Australian-built Bushmaster

Bushmaster in secondary track.

vehicles, they set them up very differently to us. Ours were full of equipment that was strapped down. This was, except for some porn magazines, generally only 'mission essential' equipment: cases of bottled water, spare machine-gun barrels and night-vision equipment. The Dutch, on the other hand, had their carpenters build cabinets into any unused space. My seat was opposite the 'coffee' cabinet. Inside was a full suite of coffee equipment: an espresso machine that they powered by an inverter from the vehicle power, a small fridge for their milk, and an array of different types of coffee. To the Dutch this was all 'mission essential' equipment.

The Dutch EOD blokes used to laugh when I travelled in their vehicle. While they jumped in and pulled off their body armour and helmets, and rarely wore seatbelts, I would get into my seat in body armour, helmet, ballistic goggles, fire retardant gloves and anti-flash hood. Once in my seat I would strap myself in as tight as I could and generally fall promptly to sleep. I have always been lucky to be able to sleep anywhere – even with the threat of having a chipboard cabinet of coffee apparatus flung at me if we hit an IED.

19

WORKING WITH COALITION FORCES

TWICE DAILY I WOULD VISIT THE AUSTRALIAN headquarters, first for the morning intelligence briefing and later for the operations brief. I would regularly brief them in turn on new insurgent trends.

When I wasn't working in the lab or writing reports, I was out visiting different groups: the Dutch brigade headquarters, which directed conventional operations in the province; the Dutch staff officers, who were, on one level, my direct superiors, but who had little interest in or influence on what my team did; and the US aviation battalion that ran the Black Hawks, Kiowas and Chinooks from the far side of the airfield.

Some of my favourite visits were to the US Special Forces guys who lived and worked nearby. I would drive to the gate of their compound in our clapped-out truck, then begin the task of getting through the multiple checkpoints manned by Afghan police. All I could do was try to explain that I was there to see

Scotty, my contact among the detachment.

'Scotty?' they'd ask.

'Yes, Scotty', I'd say.

'Scotty?'

'Yes, Scotty.'

'Scotty, OK.'

They'd mutter something into their cheap two-way radio and I'd catch 'Scotty' being said a few times.

They were always pleasant, and regularly offered to buy my watch. It usually took about ten minutes to be let through – generally after being offered some chai, their hot sweet tea, decanted into dirty, fingerprint-smeared glasses from the flasks they all carried.

After three checkpoints, I would reach the inner sanctum where the Special Forces blokes lived. All were massive guys who ate, slept, did weights and sneaked around in the night shooting people. Scotty was their 'bomb guy' and our contact. He was a young, stocky little fellow who initially came across as a bit simple. But after we got to know him better, we learnt that he was anything but.

His technical qualifications for disposing of explosives were dubious. But with his Afghan police counterparts he had recovered many IEDs, which he was always keen to get to us. He had quite a personal arsenal in his bedroom/office. There was an Uzi submachine gun, an M4 assault rifle with a second barrel and receiver with an M203 grenade launcher attachment, and numerous pistols, which sat on his coffee table next to a pile of men's fitness magazines.

Above his bed, a couple of detonators dangled from a hook on the wall; they could remove a few fingers if they went off in your hand. When I asked him why he had them in his room, he shrugged and said, 'Oh, they've been there since I got here.'

Scotty was an ally who understood technical intelligence and how important it was for us to get hold of these IEDs so we could feed our findings back into the intelligence world, and he was always very open with us, freely passing on whatever had been recovered. Once, after he returned from a trip to Kandahar down Route Bear with the Afghan police, he invited us over to take the twenty-one devices they had collected on the trip. Amazingly, the Afghan police seemed to understand exactly where the IEDs were in the road. They would stop the convoy and pull on the wire or detonating cord sticking out of the loose earth and the whole device would come out. This may have had something to do with the US policy of paying for IEDs that were handed in, one of the many friction points between the US and the Dutch, who were staunchly opposed to paying for such things.

Scotty took us to his shipping container wedged between two dirt mounds. These mounds would provide some blast protection in the event that the explosives detonated for one reason or another. When he opened the doors, we realised that it was a prudent safety measure. The inside of the metal container was lined with shelves that seemed to hold every variety of IED component. There were numerous yellow palm-oil containers filled with ammonium nitrate aluminium, a favourite homemade explosive of the insurgents because it was relatively safe to make and the chemicals were easy to come by, as ammonium nitrate is a common fertiliser and the aluminium could easily be sourced from metallic paint or even by putting chunks of aluminium in coffee grinders.

Scotty's yellow palm-oil containers had been sitting in the blistering Afghan sun and many were leaching white slurry from the caps. Besides the containers, there was a variety of explosives, detonators, pressure plates, radio-controlled triggers, and wires and cords. I had a quick look and asked Pete, a qualified EOD technician, to go in first and check if the explosives were safe . . . I was a good boss. He had a look and stuck his head out of the shipping container, saying that they wouldn't meet Australian standards but it was unlikely that anything would blow up – just 'be careful what you touch', as plenty of detonators were kicking around in there.

Scotty was more than happy for us to take what we wanted. There were some interesting switches that we hadn't seen before and a few battery packs and pressure plates that we might be able to pull prints from. We also took a tub of explosives in an unusual large clear plastic tube. It had about 20 kilograms of a white grainy powder in it, not the usual grey ammonium nitrate aluminium. Back at the lab we pulled it apart to find it had a funnel in the middle to make a crudely shaped charge, so that the force of the explosion would be focused in one direction. Similar explosive charges were used to great effect by the insurgents in Iraq for blowing holes in armoured vehicles. The good ones smuggled in from Iran had copper inserts that fired a molten jet that travelled at 2000 metres per second. It would slice through armoured vehicles, walls, limbs, anything that got in its way. This was the reason we were issued with medical tourniquets that could be applied one-handed – so, after losing a limb, you could still use the tourniquet to stop bleeding and maybe save your own life.

We were concerned that this unusual charge was the first using a new technique for targeting armoured vehicles. We did some testing and later blew it up on the range against the hull of a written-off Bushmaster armoured vehicle. Thankfully it didn't have any ability to punch a hole in the armour, nor did we see any others like it that could herald a new trend for targeting armoured vehicles in the province.

Two days after Scotty's patrol went down Route Bear, the Dutch battle-group tried it. They were not so good at identifying the bombs and got badly hit several times. They lost a couple of men and were constantly fired on from the hills as they tried to recover their vehicles. Eventually they left one of their vehicles behind and called in attack helicopters to put a couple of Hellfires into it to make sure there was nothing left for the Taliban.

It was a difficult situation with the Dutch and the US hating and distrusting each other, and the US working closely with a local warlord and police chief who most likely had a hand in attacking the Dutch convoy. In some ways I understood how the US thought: while the warlord may not have been a good guy, at least he wasn't the worst, and supporting his police brought some stability to the province. It was Afghanistan; it would never be like the US or the Netherlands or Australia. The best you could hope for was that the police and army would keep the province peaceful, even if they did it through intimidation and extortion. But the Dutch refused to accept that.

20

A DEATH – AND SOME NEAR MISSES

19 JULY 2009: *YESTERDAY MORNING, PRIVATE Warren shifted his weight while positioned behind the machine gun and triggered an anti-personnel mine that almost instantly severed his leg. The mine started an explosive chain that initiated a detonating cord leading to three 82-mm mortars that detonated under his friend, Private 'Benny' Ranaudo, killing him instantly.*

They had been in the same location for two and a half hours, providing a cordon about halfway up the Baluchi Valley, while the remainder of the company conducted a search of qalas a few hundred metres south. All the while, locals had been moving through the area, within centimetres or even millimetres of the device. A young local boy lost three toes and two other men received superficial wounds from fragmentation.

I was in Kandahar when it happened. A lieutenant colonel gave me the news: one Australian killed, one Australian 'priority one' and three local nationals wounded. I asked for his thoughts and he gave me the answer I was after: 'You should go'. Somehow the planets aligned and I was on an empty C-17 out to Tarin Kowt within the hour and back at the lab within two.

Pete and I got to the site by helicopter. We were dropped off in a cloud of dirt, and when the helicopter finally lifted off with three detainees, we found ourselves once more in an eerily quiet field with a small group of soldiers dotted in security positions in the surrounding trees and among banks and aqueduct walls. They were all very calm and at first it was difficult to imagine how that very morning this had been the site of an explosion, of shouting, panic, severed limbs and death.

Members of the section that sustained the casualties had asked to remain on task. I interviewed a few while Pete spoke to the EOD guys, who showed him where they had found Private Warren's foot. At first, speaking to the young corporal, the section commander in charge of Warren and Ranaudo, I didn't quite understand how it had occurred, how they had been in the same location for hours and how the device had been triggered by chance. The young corporal calmly talked me through the details several times. He explained that they had stepped out early that morning for a cordon-and-search operation. They had put in their security positions before sunrise so as not to alert the locals. His section had been part of the outer cordon while the Afghan soldiers searched specific qalas. Locals were moving through the area not long after they arrived, and Private Warren had been behind the machine gun with Ranaudo standing behind him when the bomb went off. He told me how they had looked at

Benny and realised there was no way he was going to be revived. It was likely he knew nothing of the blast.

I spent a few minutes sitting with the company commander, a man for whom I had a lot of respect. He answered all my questions, but I had the feeling he really needed a few minutes for quiet contemplation. To have soldiers under your command killed is something that can haunt a man for the rest of his life.

We moved back to Patrol Base Mashal, where we spent the night completing and submitting our report. Then we were driven back to Tarin Kowt where I briefed the battle-group headquarters. General Kelly was in attendance again, along with the deputy commander for Afghanistan. There were lots of questions. I also learnt that Warren had survived and was on his way to Germany.

That evening I turned in early. I'd had a broken night's sleep the night before, sleeping in the dust with dogs howling around me. I wasn't sure about the vigilance of the security piquet or how far away those fucking feral dogs were.

*

I didn't go to the ramp ceremony, the ceremony for loading coffins onto outgoing aircraft. In fact, I never went to a ramp ceremony. I thought the best way to remember the fallen was to keep working to try to stop losing soldiers. The death of Private Ranaudo gave a real urgency to what we were doing.

I had started to get obsessed by biometrics, the unique characteristics of each person that could be recorded, analysed and matched – fingerprints, iris patterns, facial geometry, DNA. One of the hardest things about a counterinsurgency fight, such as in Afghanistan, was identifying the insurgents. Most were farmers by day and occasionally set IEDs or shot at us when the conditions were in their favour. Very rarely did they show themselves. They did, however, leave clues: fingerprints on the electrical tape and other components. These could be matched with the individuals when the equipment and resources were available.

Small handheld units with cameras and fingerprint and iris scanners were what we needed, and about halfway through the tour my investigator managed to get us twenty-three such 'biometric enrolment units'. It presented a great opportunity. Widespread enrolment of the province's population would break new ground. Some in the government back home raised privacy concerns when we began enrolling local nationals, although I thought they were confused about where we were and what we were doing. With a widespread IED threat that in many circumstances was indiscriminately killing children, I said fuck privacy and sort this situation out any way you can.

The US saw it as a homeland security issue. They felt that the insurgents building bombs in Afghanistan now would be the same people building bombs in America in ten to twenty years' time.

*

As well as the ever-increasing IED incidents, there were other challenges. A Kiowa Warrior helicopter troop fired on a group of people on the southern side of Chora with Hellfire missiles. They were about a kilometre into the dasht. They fired two Hellfires, one a thermobaric. This killed two people outright and badly injured two others. One died shortly afterwards.

The US claimed that the Kiowas fired on the group as they were emplacing an IED. It got messy when the Dutch claimed that the locals were innocent. My team was told to deploy to the site. The commanding officer of the Australian battle-group called me in to express concern about the task: he felt it was a witch-hunt and the Dutch were playing politics. I said that all an investigation from my team could do was give him straight answers, but considering that the site was a day old there might not be many facts to find. He seemed happy with this and my team was stood down.

The following day, we had a call out to a site where a patrol had hit a device in Baluchi. We returned with a road convoy and I spent another night in the dirt – I couldn't sleep because of those dogs again. But I was roused at 2330 to receive an order from Regional Command, the higher headquarters in Kandahar. They wanted my team to do the exploitation of the US attack site, after all. The Dutch had been pushing for it.

We went there the following day, as it coincided with the patrol route back to Tarin Kowt, but found very little. There were obvious bloodstains and craters. It looked like one person had been melted onto his motorbike. My report said nothing but what we found: two missile impact craters, and a third crater that may have been dug by insurgents attempting to emplace an IED.

We didn't help anyone with our report . . . but we didn't condemn anyone either. I resented my team being used to try to implicate other soldiers and make political statements. Particularly when the lines between right and wrong, and who was an insurgent and who wasn't, were so blurry.

*

For a week or so in August, it seemed we were losing a vehicle a day to IED strikes in the Baluchi Valley. And there were other incidents elsewhere. The Dutch had an IED strike out near Patrol Base Tabar. The device didn't function properly, which was lucky as the soldier was only 3 metres away.

Some qualified trackers with them identified a sandal print in the dirt. They followed the prints to a nearby qala and detained a local with matching sandals. He came up positive to an explosive residue test. The device had plenty of tape to leave fingerprints on. The detainee was fingerprinted that night and the components were flown to Kandahar so the lab could pull the prints. The idea was to match them with the detainee, and hope he would be locked up for a long time. However, the prints came back negative. It was a shame – we had planned a party. But it opened a lot of people's eyes to what you could do with biometrics.

By August we were very busy. Our success meant we were never short of work and we were regularly called on at short notice to go to bomb sites. The sad reality was that there were many incidents, some days several across the province. The insurgents developed ingenious new ways to hide their bombs. They were burying them deeper so that our engineers struggled to find them with our standard mine detectors. They were covering them with plastic bowls so that a civilian vehicle wasn't heavy enough to detonate the device, but the ground pressure from a 15-tonne armoured vehicle would crush the bowl and trigger the switch underneath. Many soldiers had now been involved in numerous incidents over just a short time in Afghanistan.

One afternoon we flew out to an IED recovery. It involved an anti-handling switch designed to target EOD teams – a weight on a grenade fuse hooked up to two mortar rounds. While we were on our way back to Tarin Kowt by Black Hawk, the same patrol hit another IED as they tried to depart the location. So the next morning we were back there again. I spoke to the young driver of the vehicle that had hit the IED. He explained that the four vehicles in front of his had all turned off a secondary path onto a main track, but he had missed the turn. Not more than 5 metres further, he had hit the bomb. He also confided to me that this was his third IED strike. The blast had torn off the front wheel stations. One of the tyres could be seen about 200 metres away at the base of an almost sheer drop off the side of the spurline.

*

Not long after this, we had a night on a hill out in the Mirabad valley. An IED with a pull-string trigger had been positioned on a track to target dismounted patrols moving around the green zone.

We found the triggerman's location only about 30 metres from the impact site – very close but with the corn crops high enough that he remained well concealed.

When the Australian patrol approached, something caught the lead scout's eye. He stopped and called the section commander forward. They both looked at the string running across the track. They remained there when they saw it move, and even when the plastic insulator was pulled by the insurgent across the track in front of them. It was only later that they truly understood how close they came to being blown up.

We had a good look at the device and tried to work out why it hadn't detonated. The only thing we could see was that the connections from the battery pack to the main charge and detonator were not tight. Basically, the insurgent hadn't given the bare wires a good twist to ensure a good connection. The blokes in the patrol had been saved from serious injury by the fact that the insurgent had little understanding of basic electrical theory.

Only a few days later, we were back in Mirabad with the Dutch quick reaction force. The boys had found another IED with a pull-string. In fact, they had come across four insurgents emplacing the device. But everyone was so surprised when they came face-to-face in the head-high corn that the insurgents had got away – it would have been well within the 'rules of engagement' to shoot them on the spot. The patrol did a further search and found a second IED, then a cache of additional components in a tree.

We'd been there for about an hour and had started on the

second site when a 107-mm rocket was fired over our heads. It landed a bit further to the south, closer to where our vehicles were. We didn't stay for too much longer.

We were nearing the mid-point of our tour, and the team was starting to achieve what we'd been sent here to do. We were accepted as a group that made a valuable contribution to the overall fight in the province. The units we were supporting were better informed of the IED threat they faced. I was sure that if we kept this up, our work would be of lasting benefit to Coalition forces, the Afghan security forces and the people of Uruzgan province.

I even heard that several of our reports had made it, unedited, to the desk of the minister for defence – enough to make any staff officer proud.

21

A SUICIDE BOMBER, A HOLIDAY AND A NEW COMPONENT

THERE WAS A SUICIDE BOMBER UP IN CHORA the day before the national election in August 2009. Somehow it felt much more personal than it ever had in Baghdad. An Afghan army captain, a company commander, stopped as he drove through the bazaar. The bomber approached from an alley, shook the captain's hand, then detonated his device, killing four and badly wounding another seven.

The bomber – there was not much left of him to look at. His jaw had been shattered and rearranged so that it almost seemed as if he had teeth coming out of his forehead. His eye sockets and nose were just meaty holes on his battered face.

Hope he enjoyed his virgins.

Sometime later, a friend – the company commander from Mirwais and one of the most intelligent and professional officers I have ever worked with – was passing through Tarin Kowt and explained how well known and well liked throughout the area the

Afghan Army captain had been, particularly for his outlandish moustache with twisted ends. He recalls, macabrely, seeing his body in the makeshift morgue and thinking what a waste of an amazing moustache.

My friend also told me how he had disposed of the head and legs of the suicide bomber after we graciously refused to take them. He explained that the soldiers in the patrol base had initially been very excited that they had the head and legs of the bomber for my team. They were a little put out when my guys confirmed we had all the biometric material we needed and had no further use for the remains. I think they expected us to cold pack them and bring them back. The Afghans did not believe the bomber needed a funeral, as he had killed soldiers – they suggested he 'should be fed to the dogs'. As the Afghan locals and soldiers refused to take the remains of the suicide bomber, and the Coalition forces had nothing in place to backload such remains, the Australians in Mirwais were stuck with the bag of body bits.

My friend, the commander of the Australians on the patrol base, was faced with only one option – to bury it. So he and one other, the medic sergeant, walked up behind the patrol base to an area used as a rifle range. It was just a patch of desert on the side of a craggy mountain peak. They started to dig a small grave. The dirt was hard, having been baked in the hot Afghan sun for millennia. They chipped and chipped at the soil, but after a considerable period of time they had only been able to cut a small hollow in the hard ground.

They placed the head and legs in this small hole. They pushed and forced them in so that they could be covered with rocks, but were unable to get them to fit. My friend explained to me how he then swung his shovel at the lumps of flesh in an attempt to beat them flat in the hole. Silhouetted by the afternoon sun, high up on the hill, he swung his shovel, trying to bash the head and legs into the small scrape.

It didn't work . . . so they set fire to them. Once they had burned, he and the sergeant covered them with rocks. Every time they used the range after this, he would move a few rocks to ensure his 'little friend' had not been taken by dogs.

*

We reached halfway through the deployment. I got on a plane to Kuwait, cleaned my boots, webbing, pistol and rifle, and then took another plane to Paris to see the girls for almost two weeks. I was up all night before I flew out, driven like a crazy man to put together a report of an insurgent group that had been working in Deh Rafshan, north of Tarin Kowt. They were using artillery casings stuffed with ammonium nitrate aluminium. In the base of the device was a knot of detonating cord to set off the charge and in the mouth of the casing were packed ball bearings and other scrap metal – pretty nasty. Luckily no-one had successfully set one off yet.

When I flew out of Tarin Kowt in the C-130, my head was spinning with visions of Crystal and Eva, cold beer, and insurgent bombs and tactics. I fell asleep somewhere on the way to Kuwait, soothed by the buzz of the C-130.

The twelve days in France were like a dream. Eva had grown and Crystal was stylishly sporting a six-month pregnant belly. Our first thing to do as a couple was to open an envelope from her obstetrician that she had been carrying for weeks. Together we discovered we were having a little sister for Eva.

After a day, we fled the bustle of Paris to a sleepy little town near Limoges, about three hours south-west. In a little stone house, we picked up where we had left off. Crystal's life had been on hold since she'd moved to the Gold Coast to be near her parents. Somehow a lot of our conversation didn't connect. She wanted to tell me what had been happening in Broadbeach, and I had nothing much to tell her except stories of how Pete was afflicted by gout and I slept in a shipping container.

I had four more months in Afghanistan, so I couldn't tell Crystal that I'd been travelling through the province by helicopter and armoured vehicle. In the eight years since we'd first met, I could count the time I had been away in years, and more stress was not something she needed. I could see she was constantly anxious, and I knew not to say anything that might make that worse.

We spent lazy days driving through the French countryside and passed a night or two in a small seaside town. We had beach picnics with chicken and fresh bread and dinner in small local restaurants, which quite inexplicably always seemed to involve dishes of offal (even though what we ordered in broken French sounded quite innocent).

In the time I had been in Afghanistan, the world had embraced smart phones. Crystal's iPhone was the first I had played with, yet, incredibly, Eva at eighteen months delighted in showing me how she could unlock it and open her favourite game. I had been left behind by my toddler.

I felt physically sick as I left them at the end of the holiday. To this day, I am haunted by the image of them waving goodbye through the hotel window as I drove off to Charles de Gaulle Airport – back to a war zone, a place of suicide bombers and worse. Little Eva with a puzzled look on her face and Crystal trying hard not to cry. I couldn't get the thought out of my head: *this is crazy. Why am I leaving my two favourite people?*

I missed them so much and, as if Afghanistan knew to turn on the right weather to match my mood, it was bitterly cold when I returned to Tarin Kowt. The highest of the craggy peaks that surrounded the town had gained a fine covering of snow.

*

My first job back was to send Pete out with one of the Dutch investigators to a strike in East Deh Rafshan on 19 October. A local man had ridden over an IED on his motorbike and been killed.

The pair inspected the site, then went to Patrol Base Tabar to inspect the body. Clouds were coming over and a cold wind picked up as they unwrapped the stiff, cold corpse under torchlight in a dark shipping container. He was fairly intact. His right arm had been amputated by the blast (they had earlier found his hand at the bomb site). His leg was attached only by flaps of skin, and he had facial injuries from the blast – his eye had been pushed back into his head.

Under torchlight they stripped him to look for scars, tattoos and additional tell-tale injuries. Finding none, they started to take his fingerprints, first electronically, then with ink. The Dutchman complained as he inadvertently snapped one of the body's stiff fingers, twisting it as he tried to straighten it to get the fingerprint. In a darkly comical twist, while the two wrestled with the corpse's arms to take prints, the Dutch investigator bent over, close to the naked, rigormortic body. He took the print, then turned his head to look at the body. He was startled to find himself only a centimetre from the cold penis – he told me it was as though it was looking at him. It was grisly work, and both returned a little shaky. I made a note to keep an eye on them.

Although it took a while for us to realise it, Pete had made a significant breakthrough. At the site, he systematically searched the blast area. The absence of any obvious IED parts, besides shredded yellow palm-oil container, was not unusual, but this time he found a small piece of timber, a portion of a timber disc about 7 centimetres across, which looked like nothing of interest. Luckily, he decided to keep it. Only later, following a Special Forces raid in the northern end of Helmand province, just near the border with Uruzgan, did its significance become clear.

In Helmand, near the Kajaki Dam, the Australian Special

Forces had fought their way into a village where a known Taliban commander was staying. During the operation they found a cache of components, and among them were several triggers that we had never come across before. They were fabricated from a short section of narrow tree stump or branch. A wooden disc had been cut off the top and holes were bored through the base, into which a detonator and detonating cord were inserted. Down through the central hole a spike of timber was inserted and connected to the disc of timber, which acted as a pressure plate.

The device was triggered when a victim trod or drove over the wooden disc, which acted as a pressure plate and would push a small wooden spike into the detonator. The sensitive primary explosive would detonate, which in turn set off a reaction through the detonating cord leading to the main charge. The danger was this: if the main charge didn't have any metal content, which a lot of the home-made explosives in the yellow palm-oil containers didn't, there was nothing to find with conventional mine detectors. Most devices had some metal – engineers with basic search equipment can find firing pins in land mines, saw blades that work as contacts in pressure plates, battery packs and even wiring. But not these little fuckers – there was not a scrap of metal, so we had no way to find them with mine detectors.

For this reason, the fragment from East Deh Rafshan was a big deal and attracted a lot of attention. It was the first time such a device had been found actually emplaced. And the dead man in the shipping container was proof that it worked. We quickly wrote a report on the 'no-metal' content triggers and made some assumptions about the supply chain from Helmand to East Deh Rafshan. Not long afterwards we found out that one of the Dutch battalions was planning a cordon and search operation based on our report.

In a rush, the trigger captured by the Special Forces was sent to a lab in Bagram, near Kabul, for analysis. While examining one of the detonators, an overly enthusiastic scientist, in his haste, punctured the plastic case around the explosive with his metal probe. This instantly detonated the small cylinder, which blew several of his fingers off, and delayed any further analysis of the remaining detonators.

*

Well before winter set in, I had decided we needed some fun, and had come up with a plan to pinch a big steel stove made from welded wheel hubs. Nobody seemed too interested in the stove where it sat outside the Australian headquarters, but we figured that it would be highly sought after once the weather cooled down. We had also just been given some hardwood that the chippies – carpenters from the Australian construction engineers – didn't need.

So the four of us spent a couple of hours one evening covertly reconnoitring the location of the stove within the inner secure compound, planning how to get it through a gap we had found in the fence, then another hour picking the right time to roll the stove from where it sat, out of the compound and into the back of our old truck.

With our new stove in the truck, we drove back to the lab and soon had it in place. It had been a successful team-building and stress-relieving activity. With our newly acquired hardwood planks, the stove kept us very warm over the winter and was extremely good for destroying classified documents.

*

Journal entry, 9 November 2009: *Prime Minister in today. Didn't see him. Made a nuisance of himself.*

Soon came Eid, a Muslim holiday for the locals. I knocked the blokes off early, as it was the local custom to fire rifles into the air in celebration. It was difficult to explain to them that bullets come down almost as fast as they go up. I was not keen for my blokes to be sitting in our unprotected office all evening while the bullets randomly fell. As we left the dining hall following dinner, snakes of machine-gun tracer streamed through the air overhead.

After six months in Afghanistan, I could see the team was starting to tire. I was feeling it myself. We were doing long days – fourteen-hour days, seven days a week. But the job kept driving us onwards, and little victories kept us happy.

22

SEEING THE BIG PICTURE

IT TOOK ME ALMOST SIX MONTHS TO UNDERstand what it was all about in Afghanistan. Somehow I'd got so wound up about the bombs that I hadn't taken the time to understand what the soldiers were achieving. It took a four-day stopover in a remote patrol base to open my eyes.

On 11 November, a strike injured one Australian and three Afghan army soldiers. I was picked up at the back gate of the command post and we drove straight to the landing zone, swearing at people who got in our way. Two medivac helicopters were sitting with their rotors turning when we arrived. After speaking with the loadmaster and convincing him that we needed to be on the flight (and lying a little by telling him we were authorised to be on it), we were directed onto a Black Hawk. It was empty in the back except for three closed stretchers and medical gear in backpacks. In a second we were up and flying over Tarin Kowt towards West Deh Rafshan.

We touched down in a field and the loadmasters threw open the doors. After the turmoil of loading casualties onto the helicopter, including the injured Australian soldier giving permission for his mates to use his bodybuilding supplements, the helicopter took off in a storm of dust, and we got on with the job.

The calm after the strike.

One of the injured Afghans had refused to get on the helicopter and was limping around, and the Afghan patrol commander beat two suspects with a shovel before the young Australian lieutenant could stop him.

Once we had gathered the evidence we needed and taken enough pictures of the bomb site, we headed over the river towards Patrol Base Buman, which was home for these Afghan and Australian soldiers. The mainly Afghan patrol all moved at a fast pace and, although I was in good shape (and Pete had recovered from his gout), it was not long before we started to hurt. I was wearing heavy body armour and carrying my pack, rifle and helmet for the hour-or-so walk back to the base. The Afghan soldiers skipped along with just a rifle and a few magazines or an RPG and a couple of spare rockets.

Conditions at Buman were comfortable, but with few luxuries. The boys slept, did weights, went on patrol, or trained the Afghans. The day after we arrived, they were out patrolling the same ground. The Australian lieutenant spent some time convincing his Afghan counterpart that this was the right thing to do. Get out and show the locals and the insurgents that the Afghan army still owned the ground. That it took more than a bomb blast and a few injured to confine them to their base.

I was in awe of the courage and stoicism of the team. They had taken casualties the day before, but out they went, knowing they had very little to protect themselves from hidden bombers, who waited and watched as they approached. They had to trust that their body armour, helmets, well-practised drills, reliance on each other – and a degree of luck – would protect them.

That night, after we returned from the patrol, just on dusk, we tramped out to the 'burn pit' near the row of concertina wire that marked the boundaries of the base. All rubbish was burned during a Friday-night ritual at the pit. Helped along by 40 litres of diesel, the flames leapt out in bursts that must have been visible all over Deh Rafshan. It was as though we were making a further statement to the locals that we were there. When the flames finally died, we all tramped back behind the Hesco walls.

For four days I watched this small team of Australians – a young lieutenant and an older warrant officer, a handful of infantry, an artillery forward observer and a medic – train the Afghan soldiers, negotiate patrols, coax and coach them out the gate of the patrol base. There was mutual respect. The Australians understood the reality for the Afghan soldiers – that the countryside was full of Taliban who wanted to kill them. And the Afghan soldiers understood that the Australians were here risking their lives to help them keep the country from falling into the hands of their enemy.

I was thankful that we had upset the Dutch operations staff by jumping in the medivac helicopter without permission – it gave us a privileged insight into a small part of the lives of these Australian soldiers on the front line.

But as payback the Dutch operations staff failed to organise a return trip for us.

*

Once finally back in Tarin, after our four days at Patrol Base Buman, there was a four-day backlog of work for me and Pete to get stuck into. We were invited to the Afghan army compound to see items recovered on a recent operation. The Australian mentors and Afghan soldiers had found some large caches in Mirabad, including nearly sixty PG-7 rounds, a B-10 recoilless rifle with four rounds, plus a few IED switches that no-one thought much of.

We turned up with an Australian captain and an interpreter, and when the trunks of PG-7 rounds were pulled out, all the Afghan soldiers crowded around – there must have been fifty, all up. Most were small, simple-looking men who came up to my shoulder, but one or two fitted the 'Russian rape-baby' profile: they were a little taller than the rest, with light-brown hair and blue eyes.

An Afghan captain was obviously concerned that we were there to take his prize, the B-10 recoilless rifle. Although a clunky old weapon, it was a Taliban status symbol. Pete started examining the rounds to see if they were worth keeping and luckily instantly attracted the attention of most of the Afghan soldiers.

The ammunition was old and corroded to the point that you could put your finger through many of the light alloy cones on the nose of the rockets. Pete sorted them into a large pile to be disposed of and a small pile of six to keep. The Afghan soldiers were confused about which pile was which – they wanted to keep most.

I quietly took off away from the crowd with a small bag of switches I had found at the bottom of one trunk. There was an improvised 'peg' switch, two new anti-handling switches and wooden pieces to fabricate more – quite a find.

The Afghan battalion executive officer came over and made a nuisance of himself but in the end allowed us to take the switches and dispose of the corroded PG-7 rounds. We left after much hand-shaking and a promise that we would return to give a presentation on how the switches worked. But I knew we would never explain to this crowd of Afghan soldiers exactly how to build an IED.

The whole experience was a great insight into the Afghan battalions – the officers were all about keeping face, while the soldiers were poorly educated and poorly trained, but had a child-like enthusiasm you couldn't help but warm to. They were never going to be a fighting force that would rival a Western, First World army. But the training and mentoring they were getting from the Coalition forces in the province was good. I felt there was a better than average chance they could hold the Taliban at bay after we withdrew at the end of 2013, or at the very least help force them to the bargaining table. Only time would tell.

*

Not long after this, we flew out to an IED find in the Baluchi Valley. It was another opportunity to see the work the Australians were doing. We were dropped in a field and led through a maze of qalas, not far from where Private Ranaudo was killed. While we waited for the Dutch EOD team, who were walking in from the dasht, I exchanged pleasantries with the patrol commander, a matter-of-fact 50-year-old who was somewhat of a legend in the infantry corps for his years of training jungle warfare – Jungle Jim, he was affectionately called.

It wasn't long before the Dutch team leader, Attila, and his men arrived. It was all smiles and handshakes. He and his partner were a funny pair – both Dutch gypsies. Attila was a burly buck-toothed bear of a man, while his partner was slight and quiet. Both were well-known and well-liked by the Australians.

Attila made some final equipment checks. Then, no longer smiling, he walked stoically towards the small sack with wires emerging from it that the patrol had identified. We all waited behind cover, in case Attila didn't get it right.

After a small bang, when Attila cut the battery wires with a detonator, he called us forward. We recovered the remnants of the radio-controlled IED with four 82-mm mortar rounds.

Two days later, we were back there again: the same patrol had found two IEDs within 150 metres of each other, and one had just detonated. It had been emplaced on the bank of a deep aqueduct, where one of the Australian sections had moved after they found the first device. From speaking to the section commander, I learnt he must have unknowingly stepped over it while looking for a spot to go to the toilet. When they switched off their radio-controlled IED jammer, it had blown – amazingly, there had been no casualties.

The first IED was a large radio-controlled bomb consisting of about 12 kilograms of homemade explosive mixed with small motorcycle parts (added for fragmentation). While we were looking at it, the patrol commander got a call to investigate another suspicious item.

It was a long walk with our gear, including the bag of ammonium nitrate aluminium full of ball bearings, and nuts and bolts in my small pack. Then, when we arrived, the suspicious item was gone. The patrol questioned some locals and sprayed several with X-Spray to see if they had been handling explosives. In the end they had six suspects: shady-looking men. Using my biometrics kit, I recorded photos, fingerprints and irises, and noted their names, where they were picked up, where they were from and so on.

They were detained and marched back to the base, where one started to bleat after a little questioning. He claimed one of the others was Taliban and had recovered the IED and emplaced it in another location.

We sat at Patrol Base Mashal for three days, waiting for a return flight. It was freezing cold and the only accommodation was a canvas tent that had bent poles so the flaps wouldn't close; the wind whistled through the place all night. I only had what I carried in my small pack, and I had left room for evidence, so that wasn't much at all. In my lightweight sleeping bag and thermal shirt and trousers, I froze and got bugger-all sleep. I was an idiot and a touch too proud to ask the men based there for more gear.

While we waited, the detainees were released, as they had reached the maximum detention period without charge. The Black Hawks kept circling, but never landed. But at least I got to watch Jim and his team at work. It was inspiring to see how he led his patrol out into the thick fog that blanketed the Baluchi Valley one morning. I wasn't keen to get out of bed, but Jim rallied the Afghan soldiers, motivated his team, and off they trudged out the gate of the patrol base. Hours later, they returned, wet and cold, to hot soup the patrol base cook had ready for them.

*

Journal entry: *At least eleven killed today. Eight Afghan soldiers just outside Patrol Base Mashal. Soldiers who I had lived alongside and patrolled with just after Christmas. Another three Afghan police were killed near Patrol Base Tabar.*

*

By mid-January we were preparing to go home. I realised how long we had been there when Scotty, the US Special Forces bomb guy, who had rotated out two months after we arrived, now rotated back to the province after a four-month break stateside. The roles had reversed and somehow we were the experienced guys telling him what was going on in the province.

We had formalised the process for requesting helicopter movements for teams like ours and cut through a lot of the red tape and bureaucracy. There was now a form to submit for requesting transport out to a bomb site. It wasn't perfect, but we left the problem better than we found it.

We had finally convinced our Dutch weapons intelligence counterparts to work after dinner rather than watch movies and do 'shportz' (go to the gym in lime-green bike pants, ride slowly on an exercise bike for 15 minutes, then talk for an hour beside the water fridge). While they were reasonable characters, initially they didn't grasp the bigger picture, didn't see that the work they were doing would save lives. I think they finally started to listen by the time we left. It was the rollover after an IED attack near Tabar that turned one of them – it had been his friend who was crushed when the vehicle flipped.

On my second-last day in town, I made my farewells at the Australian headquarters, and the commanding officer said some very kind words at his nightly briefing. Perhaps my memory has embellished them somewhat, but I recall him saying: 'It would be difficult to understand how far behind we would be without a team like yours keeping a check on the IED threat. While we do not know for sure, your team has likely been responsible for saving lives, more so than all the individuals in this room together.' I passed the sentiment on to the rest of my team, who grinned at me – we had done what we had gone there to do.

*

Journal entry, 3 February 2010: *On the flight home after three days in Dubai. Still constantly checking my hip for my pistol, which I returned to the armoury days ago.*

This homecoming will be very different. In 2004, after two days at the Coalition hospital in Baghdad, then a week in a US hospital in Germany, I arrived at Sydney airport and was wheeled out through a back entrance to a waiting car, where I was whisked out to the military hospital in Holsworthy. During the drive a radio reporter announced that I had arrived back in Australia.

This homecoming will also be very different to the reception at Sydney airport when we arrived home in 2006. Then, there were reporters, cameras and a grieving widow. Today I don't expect to be met at the airport. Rather I will have a shuttle bus drop me to the girls. This is fitting.

I break into a smile every now and then when I think of the work we have done and what we have achieved. Somehow I feel that I have quieted those demons somewhat and done my part to stop soldiers and locals from being injured or killed.

EPILOGUE

I WAS HOME TO MY BEAUTIFUL CRYSTAL, WHO was right on nine months. Through all this time, she'd been raising little Eva on her own, while steadily getting more and more pregnant. Eva was sheepish around me for the first few hours after I arrived by shuttle bus to the apartment on the Gold Coast.

'Decompression' is compulsory when a soldier returns from overseas deployment. The idea is sound: it's not healthy to go from long periods in a war zone straight to a long holiday. The large battalions and company groups had a process: set programs, including time with psychs, a bit of team bonding, a few social functions and the opportunity to have a beer or ten. The idea was that it was better for returning soldiers to get on the piss with the blokes they deployed with rather than go home to the family to get drunk and unleash whatever built-up angst they had accumulated over the past eight months.

For smaller groups like my team, it wasn't so clear-cut. Most of us went back to work for a week, had a few short days, answered some very old emails and knocked off about lunchtime. But because the girls had moved up to the Gold Coast, I didn't have that option. Instead, I organised a day at the intelligence training centre at Canungra, in the hills behind the Gold Coast. I gave a presentation on technical intelligence and what we had done in Afghanistan.

The presentation was somewhat inconsequential. Afterwards, I left the secure area and picked up my mobile phone, to find I had a couple of missed calls. I phoned Crystal back, who told me she thought I should come home, as she was pretty sure she was having contractions.

Four days after I returned from Afghanistan, lovely little Zoe was born.

*

Our family moved to Townsville and I spent two years at the Combat Training Centre there. I couldn't have asked for a more rewarding role. For the first year, I was a mentor for commanders about to deploy overseas. Throughout their training, I would be their shadow and make sure they got the most from it. I would be a sounding board and advisor, but more importantly I would pull together 'after-action reviews' so that they could understand how they performed – what they did well and what they could improve on.

In the second year, the commanding officer appointed me lead planner of the large exercises: multi-million dollar activities that I designed and ran, involving a couple of thousand people, including people from AusAID and the Department of Foreign Affairs and Trade through to the federal police and the air force F/A-18s. There were thousands of moving parts, but most importantly I was given the flexibility to design exercises so that what I had learnt overseas was transferred on through the training. I had a chance to pass on the lessons I had learnt about getting blown up, developing technical intelligence and biometrics, and some of the things I had gathered, particularly from Afghanistan, about counterinsurgency warfare. It was a great posting to have after a long deployment.

It was during this period that I was told I had been selected to command a squadron in my old regiment. Squadron command was seen as the pinnacle of a junior officer's career. I was promoted to major in the field by a general and posted up to lead A Squadron, back with the 2nd Cavalry Regiment.

I really enjoyed working with soldiers again. Perhaps, though, squadron command didn't live up to its reputation as the pinnacle of roles. Perhaps after seventeen years in the army, the difficult parts of the job were becoming harder and harder to tolerate. Perhaps I struggled to give all I could to the role and the 120 officers and soldiers under my command. During this time I spent four months away training in Shoalwater Bay – it was another chunk missed of Eva's life, and now Zoe was growing up too.

Things came to a head when, nearing the end of my first year as squadron commander, I was put under pressure to go back to Afghanistan. The job was a good one – head of plans for the province – but my heart wasn't in it. There was no way I could leave the girls again, particularly as the army couldn't give me a firm end-date for the deployment – it was supposed to be nine months but might stretch to twelve months or longer, as it was likely to cover the Australian draw-down and exit.

So – for the first time in my career – I said no, I would not volunteer for the job. My commanding officer threatened that my career would suffer and that I would not be considered for the next promotion gate, selection for Command and Staff College, which meant I would stagnate at my current rank. His point was that I was not offering 'effective' service by failing to fill a service need – and on one level I completely agreed with him.

I went home and discussed it with Crystal and she was clear: 'I think it's time you got out of the army.' This was something she had never said to me before, although I was sure she had wanted to. My life in the service had taken a toll on her. I had been away from her for years, and Eva, aged 5, had already moved house five times. It wasn't fair on them; while it hurt to walk away from a career to which I had given so much, I knew my family had to take precedence – a very overdue sentiment on my part.

I left the military wanting to find a worthwhile job where I wouldn't have to sell my soul, and where I would be doing something ethically grounded. It took a while to find it. I eventually found a good job with an employer who had the foresight to see what a former military person could bring to his organisation. I had been appalled by how far from reality was the private-sector rhetoric that employers would jump at the chance to get someone from the military. I was equally sickened by the mantra for motivating staff in many management roles: 'That's how you get the big house in Mosman.'

*

As I write, Iraq is again plunged into war. My dream of going back to a peaceful Baghdad – boating on the Tigris, lazy afternoons in restaurants lining the boulevards near the 14th July Monument – now seem more distant than ever. The Islamic State fighters have orchestrated the perfect inducement to draw the attention of the Western world. By beheading journalists, they have put the media in a frenzy. The West has allowed the media to posture, and to drive popular opinion – and so it is inevitable that once more we are dropping bombs and deploying 'advisers' into the war zones of Iraq and Syria.

While I don't necessarily disagree with responding aggressively to the advance of the Islamic State, I can't help but feel we have taken the bait of the extremists. By committing forces to fight them, we have legitimised their cause. The prestige of opposing Western forces has given a significant boost to both the reach and numbers of Islamic State recruitment. Most alarmingly, as arrests and shootings continue around Australia, there now appears some truth to the prediction that home-grown terror cells and returning radicalised foreign fighters will be the greatest threat to Western countries in the near future.

The biggest mistake anyone can make, assessing this whole tragic episode in global affairs, is to believe that it is more ideologically or religiously based than it is. This is not a Muslim versus Christian fight. Nor is it even Sunni versus Shia, or Kurd. And it is definitely not an Arab versus the West fight. Rather this is a fight against a group of arseholes for whom religion is just an excuse to spread their influence by force, carrying out wanton atrocities as they see fit.

*

In April 2014 there were several television reports about a former soldier, Matthew Millhouse, and his fight with younger onset dementia. Matt served with me in Iraq and his illness has been linked to the IED attack in which we were both wounded.

My wounds were obvious and I was treated with surgery and hospitalisation; Matt's wounds were not obvious, but were much worse and much more sinister. Matt has suffered from depression, post-traumatic stress and now dementia. He only received treatment years later, when his condition became debilitating. His current state is such that he has been admitted to a nursing home because his young family is no longer able to look after him. He is 34 years old.

I owe Matt a lot. He helped protect me when I was injured in the streets of Baghdad, when I couldn't protect myself. He assisted in my evacuation to hospital. He sat by my bed when I was in recovery after surgery.

Like all of the men from my old troop, I was gutted by news of his illness, as well as being quietly concerned that my mind, too, could start to tune out, any day now.

I visited Matt in July 2014. He had trouble walking and speaking clearly. His partner told me that his condition is deteriorating quickly and she notices weekly changes. It appears that the bomb blast I survived in Iraq will kill a soldier, but many years later than anyone expected.

I finished writing this memoir only a few months before the tenth anniversary of the IED attack in Baghdad and about eighteen months after leaving the army. The Governor-General has invited my patrol to morning tea at Admiralty House, Kirribilli, for the anniversary, and we're planning to have a few beers afterwards.

ACKNOWLEDGEMENTS

A few individuals are cast in a bad light in this book. I acknowledge it is easy for me to sit in my quiet back room and criticise actions or attitudes. Most I have not named because, really, I don't have a personal gripe with you; rather, I deplore the circumstances and the system that allowed you to do, and get away with, what you did. If any of you feel that I have incorrectly portrayed you or your actions, I strongly encourage you to contact me to discuss this, or – better still – write something that tells your side of the story. The more we tell our stories, the more the public will understand the tensions, inherent contradictions and realities of life for Australians in modern war zones.

Those I have named are high-profile figures; trying to conceal their identities would have been futile and would have undermined the points I was trying to make.

To borrow the words of the wise sergeant mentioned in Part 2, Trent Morris: 'Everyone makes mistakes. I make them every day.'

I really do make mistakes every day. And, regretfully, I have also had to deal with other people's mistakes; to omit them from my account would have detracted from its truthfulness. While some of my opinions may have softened over the last few years, writing a book with deliberate omissions designed to protect the feelings of a handful of people was something I could never do.

Now, to switch tack – there are many people I must thank.

First, thank you to everyone who played a part in saving my life in 2004: the members of SECDET V, particularly the cavalry troop and attachments, who protected their injured troop leader and got him to hospital; the medical staff at the CSH and Landstuhl; and all those who played a part in my evacuation back to Australia. Once back in Sydney, I was lucky enough to be operated on by Dr Antonio Fernandes and his team, whose talent and skills produced a great result despite a shabby canvas on which to paint.

Thank you to my father, who, armed only with a sharp mind and a credit card, challenged the diplomats and Defence hierarchy to ensure that I made it back to Australia when they were found to be lacking a plan.

And, of course, thank you to my exceptional wife, Crystal – my nurse, my best friend and a young woman who, like so many other Defence partners, has been forced to live with an absentee partner during prolonged deployments. Crystal, thank you for everything you have put up with. From now on the only adventures I will have, we'll have together. Love you.

Additionally, thank you to our gracious host for the tenth

anniversary of the IED strike, General Sir Peter Cosgrove, the Governor-General. Also, warm thanks to both the Victorian and Tasmanian RSLs for providing financial support for those attending the event.

It would be remiss of me not to mention those who have played important parts in the writing of this book.

To Gillian Delbridge, my mother, whom I forced, time and time again, to live through the stories of her son in a war zone, as she helped review and edit my manuscript: thanks, Mum – you have been my safety blanket and secret weapon throughout. And to my wonderful sisters, Nathalie, Elspeth and Marlee, who have each, in their own way, played a part in these stories.

And, of course, thank you to my amazing daughters, Eva, Zoe and Amelia. What some term the 'armoured corps curse' – having only daughters due to working with high-powered radios inside large steel boxes on wheels – I don't see as any curse at all. To Amelia – little lady, you were born well after I wrote the journal that is the basis for this memoir, and I am so glad I haven't missed any of your life to date.

James Brown, my friend and the author of *Anzac's Long Shadow*, has not only been the catalyst for getting this book published, but has also been a tremendous support through the publication process. He also introduced me to Chris Feik and his team at Black Inc., who have been pivotal in helping turn my ramblings into something worth reading, and getting it to print.

Jim Culloden, a talented photographer and all-round good

bloke, must be thanked for allowing the use of some of his images, particularly that shot of the goat.

I have been humbled by the involvement of Major Generals Jim Molan and John Cantwell. Both have challenged my thinking and at times, quite rightly, put a snotty-nosed major in his place. Thank you, gentlemen, for your candour and support.

Defence has been very gracious in reviewing my manuscript and providing some leniency in allowing me to tell the stories as completely as I wished.

To my extended family, the men and women of the 2nd Cavalry Regiment, 2nd/14th Light Horse, SECDETs V and IX, and my Weapons Intelligence Team, it has been an honour and a privilege working with all of you over the years.

Kyle Tyrrell, the Boss, Officer Commanding SECDET IX, must receive a particular acknowledgement. His inspirational leadership, selfless service and personal sacrifice – and the systemic failure to support him – is a story all Australian military commanders must learn from. It does not get said enough – on behalf of the men and women of SECDET IX, thank you, Boss.

To Beau St Leone – in my eyes the quintessential modern Australian soldier – thank you for letting me use your personal story and tell of your classic Australian larrikin personality. I truly hope that the Army gets over its current agenda to be an institution for Australian social reform and instead understands that you cannot send a man to a war zone, to survive and thrive amid violence and death, and then expect him to return home and be 'normal'. When this change finally comes around, I hope to see Beau in the running for Regimental Sergeant Major of the Army.

Matthew and Terese Millhouse, the two bravest people I know, thank you. Australia needs to thank you. None of us can really fathom what you are going through or will go through. I hope telling your story draws a little more public attention to your battle.

Lastly, to the soldiers who didn't make it and therefore cannot read, or critique, what I have written – Jake Kovco, Jamie Bodley and Benny Ranaudo, to name only a few – I hope I have done your stories credit. And to their families – I hope I have shown your young men in an appropriate light.

Garth Callender

April 2015